Building Wireless
Community Networks

SECOND EDITION

Building Wireless Community Networks

Rob Flickenger

O'REILLY®

Beijing · Cambridge · Farnham · Köln · Paris · Sebastopol · Taipei · Tokyo

Building Wireless Community Networks, Second Edition
by Rob Flickenger

Copyright © 2003, 2002 O'Reilly & Associates, Inc. All rights reserved.
Printed in the United States of America.

Published by O'Reilly & Associates, Inc., 1005 Gravenstein Highway North,
Sebastopol, CA 95472.

O'Reilly & Associates books may be purchased for educational, business, or sales pro-
motional use. Online editions are also available for most titles (*safari.oreilly.com*). For
more information, contact our corporate/institutional sales department: (800) 998-9938
or *corporate@oreilly.com*.

Editor:	Mike Loukides
Production Editor:	Philip Dangler
Cover Designer:	Ellie Volckhausen
Interior Designer:	David Futato

Printing History:

January 2002:	First Edition.
June 2003:	Second Edition.

0-596-00502-4

[C]

Table of Contents

Preface

Building Wireless Community Networks is about getting people connected to one another. Wireless technology is being used right now to connect neighborhoods, businesses, and schools to the vast and nebulous entity known as the Internet. One of the goals of this book is to help you get your community "unplugged" and online, using inexpensive off-the-shelf equipment.

A secondary, but critical goal of this book is to come to terms with exactly what is meant by *community*. It might refer to your college campus, where many people own their own laptops and want to share files and access to the Internet. Your idea of community could encompass your apartment building or neighborhood, where broadband Internet access may not even be available. This book is intended to get you thinking about what is involved in getting people in your community connected together, and it will demonstrate working examples of how to make these connections possible.

New in This Edition

The most important addition to this book is the inclusion of Tim Pozar's excellent paper, "Regulations Affecting 802.11 Deployment." Tim is a microwave communications engineer and ham radio operator, and he has done terrific work in exploring the labyrinthine FCC Part 15 regulations. His paper helps us all to understand exactly what is required to operate wireless equipment legally in the United States.

I will also take a look at relevant technologies that have recently entered the wireless networking world, including 802.11a, 802.11g, and 802.1x. While 802.11b is still widely regarded as the champion technology of the community wireless networking effort, these newer technologies are poised to bring interesting new capabilities to networking projects everywhere.

In addition, I discuss a number of fun new home-brew equipment and software designs that have come to light, and evaluate some new security tools (and challenges). In particular, the Host AP driver has graduated to near-production quality, and can provide a very flexible alternative to traditional APs. More on that later.

Audience

This book describes some solutions to the current (but rapidly changing) problem of building an open wireless network for community use. It is *not* intended to be a design guide for wireless companies and ISPs, though I hope they find the information in it useful (and at least a little bit entertaining).

This book is intended for the technical user who is interested in bringing wireless high-speed network access to wherever it's needed. This could include extending Internet connectivity to areas where other types of access (such as DSL and cable) aren't available. It might also include setting up access at a school, where structures were built long before anyone thought about running cables and lines into classrooms. This book should also be useful for people interested in learning about how dozens of groups around the planet are providing wireless access in their own communities. The story of wireless network access is still in its infancy, but is already full of fascinating twists and turns (never mind its potential!). I hope to communicate what I've learned of this story to you.

Organization

Early chapters of this book introduce basic wireless concepts and essential network services, while later chapters focus on specific aspects of building your own wireless network. Experienced users may prefer to skip around rather than read this book from cover to cover, so here's an overview of each chapter:

- Chapter 1, *Wireless Community Networks*, gives a brief history of the state of wireless connectivity, and some ideas (and warnings) about how things might proceed.

- Chapter 2, *Defining Project Scope*, is an overview of many important logistical considerations you will face in designing your own network, and describes some tools that may make your job easier.

- Chapter 3, *Network Layout*, provides a detailed description of critical network components that you will need to provide your users. Network design and security considerations are also addressed.

- Chapter 4, *Using Access Points*, details how to use Wireless Access Point hardware effectively in your networking project.

- Chapter 5, *Host-Based Networking*, is a step-by-step guide to building your own Access Point using Linux, inexpensive PC hardware, and conventional wireless client cards.

- Chapter 6, *Long-Range Networking*, is about extending your range. It looks at using topographic mapping software to evaluate long distance links, and examines the myriad antennas, cables, connectors you are likely to encounter. It also provides a simple method for calculating the usable range of your gear.

- Chapter 7, *Other Applications*, investigates some really exotic (and useful!) applications of 802.11b. It includes practical pointers for setting up point-to-point links, some simple repeaters, assembling a 2.4GHz antenna from ordinary household objects, and lots of other fun hackery. We'll also see an implementation of a dynamic "captive portal" firewall using open source (*http://www.opensource.org*) software.

- Chapter 8, *Radio Free Planet*, is a resource guide to some of the major players in the wireless network access revolution. Here you'll find out how people all over the globe are making ubiquitous wireless network access a reality, all in their free time.

- Chapter 9, *Radio Free Sebastopol*, is the (brief) history of my own experiences in setting up a wireless community network in Sebastopol, CA (and in meeting directly with the heads of some of the biggest community efforts in the U.S.).

- Appendix A contains Tim Pozar's paper, "Regulations Affecting 802.11 Deployment."

- Appendix B provides a path loss calculation table.

- Appendix C offers a shell script that makes network scheme management easier.

Typographical Conventions

The following typographical conventions are used in this book:

Italic
> Used to introduce new terms, to indicate URLs, variables or user-defined files and directories, commands, file extensions, filenames, directory or folder names, and UNC pathnames.

`Constant italic`
> Used to show variables for which a context-specific substitution should be made.

 Indicates a tip.

 Indicates a warning.

Comments and Questions

Please address comments and questions about this book to the publisher:

O'Reilly & Associates, Inc.
1005 Gravenstein Highway North
Sebastopol, CA 95472
(800) 998-9938 (in the United States or Canada)
(707) 829-0515 (international/local)
(707) 829-0104 (fax)

There is a web page for this book, which lists errata, examples, or any additional information. You can access this page at:

http://www.oreilly.com/catalog/wirelesscommnet2

To comment or ask technical questions about this book, send email to:

bookquestions@oreilly.com

For more information about books, conferences, Resource Centers, and the O'Reilly Network, see the O'Reilly web site at:

http://www.oreilly.com

Acknowledgments

I would like to thank the O'Reilly Network Team, my parents, and especially Cat for their endless encouragement and keeping me sane (and, in some cases, even sensible).

Also, my sincere thanks to Schuyler Erle, Adam Flaherty, Nate Boblitt, and Jim Rosenbaum for helping to turn the NoCat idea into an actual living project. Thanks as well to Matt Peterson, Matt Westervelt, Adam Shand, Terry Schmidt, and the countless other pioneers of ultra-hyper-connectivity.

Thanks go to the reviewers who read early drafts and made comments: Mike Bertsch, Simson Garfinkel, Justin Lancaster, Nicholas Maddix, and Matt Peterson. Thanks also go to all the people at O'Reilly & Associates who turned this manuscript into a finished book.

## CHAPTER 1

Wireless Community Networks

A year is an eternity in networking.
—Anonymous

In the time since the first edition of this book was published, millions of wireless networking components have shipped into the eagerly waiting hands of consumers. We've seen consumer-grade wireless equipment prices fall dramatically as more and more manufacturers integrate wireless into their own products. Articles about various aspects of wireless networking have made international news, including strange tales of WarChalking, WarDriving, and Pringles can–wielding Secret Service agents (as reported at *http://www.securityfocus.com/news/899*). Wireless access is now available in many coffeehouses, parks, schools, offices, and homes.

What is it about wireless networking that has so many people worked into such a frenzy? I believe that people's fascination with wireless is simple to understand. Wireless data networking is probably the most "magical" technology to evolve in recent times. Think of it: by installing an inexpensive PC card, your laptop can suddenly send and receive data at a very high speed, to anyone in range, even through walls! Many laptops have dispensed with the PC card altogether, and seem to magically just "be" online. Combined with the power of the Internet, your tiny battery-powered computer can now communicate globally, wherever an otherwise invisible wireless network happens to exist. More than any other networking technology, people just think it's *cool* to use wireless (never mind that it is extremely useful, cheap, and can do things that wired networks will never be able to do).

In the past year and a half, we have also seen more than a few wireless start-ups come and go. Wireless networking may be cheap and easy for the individual, but it has certainly proven to be far from a "slam-dunk" business for would-be wireless ISPs. In the same time period, the project list at

PersonalTelco (available on their site at *http://www.personaltelco.net/index. cgi/WirelessCommunities*) has grown to five times the size, now listing over 250 active community networking efforts. While public wireless networks haven't yet proven to be a stunning commercial success, *something* is certainly happening with wireless. This book is an exploration of many aspects of that something.

Why Now?

In recent times, the velocity of technology development has exceeded "blur" and is now moving at speeds that defy description. Internet technology in particular has made astounding strides in the last few years. Where only a few short years ago 56Kbps modems were all the rage, many tech heads now find themselves complaining about how slow their company's T1 connection seems compared to their 6MBps DSL connection at home.

Never before have so many had free and fast access to so much information. As more people get a taste of millisecond response times and megabit download speeds, they seem to only hunger for more. In most places, the service that everyone is itching for is *DSL*, or *Digital Subscriber Line* service. It provides relatively high bandwidth (anywhere from 128Kbps to 6Mbps) over standard copper telephone lines, *if* your installation is within about three miles of the telephone company's CO, or central office (this is a technical constraint of the technology). DSL is generally preferred over cable modems, because a DSL connection provides guaranteed bandwidth (at least to the telephone company) and thus is not directly affected by the traffic habits of everyone else in your neighborhood. It isn't cheap (ranging anywhere from $40 to $300 per month, plus ISP and equipment charges), but that doesn't seem to be discouraging demand.

Telephone companies, of course, are completely enamored with this state of affairs. In fact, the intense demand for high-bandwidth network access has led to so much business that enormous lead times for DSL installations are the rule in many parts of the country. In many areas, if you live outside of the perceived "market" just beyond range of the CO, lead times are sometimes quoted at "two to three years" (marketing jargon for "never, but we'll take your money anyway if you like"). Worse than that, in the wake of widespread market consolidation, some customers who were quite happy with their DSL service are finding themselves stranded when their local ISP goes out of business.*

---

* One currently circulating meme deems a stranded customer "Northpointed," in honor of the ISP NorthPoint.net, which went out of business in March of 2001, leaving thousands without access.

What are the alternatives for people who desire high-speed Internet access, but aren't willing to wait for companies to package a solution for them? The telephone companies own the copper, and the cable companies own the coax.

Community wireless networks now provide easy, inexpensive, high-bandwidth network services for anyone who cares to participate.

Approved in 1997 by the IEEE Standards Committee, the 802.11 specification details the framework necessary for a standard method of wireless networked communications. It uses the 2.4GHz microwave band designated for low-power, unlicensed use by the FCC in the U.S. in 1985. 802.11 provided for network speeds of one or two megabits, using either of two incompatible encoding schemes: Frequency Hopping Spread Spectrum (FHSS), or Direct Sequence Spread Spectrum (DSSS).

In September of 1999, the 802 committee extended the specification, deciding to standardize on DSSS. This extension, 802.11b, allowed for new, more exotic encoding techniques. This pushed up the throughput to a much more respectable 5.5 or 11Mbps. While breaking compatibility with FHSS schemes, the extensions made it possible for new equipment to continue to interoperate with older 802.11 DSSS hardware. The technology was intended to provide "campus" access to network services, allowing a typical range of about 1,500 feet. As we'll see in Chapter 2, a few new important protocols have been approved that push available wireless bandwidth even higher: all the way up to 54Mbps (but more on that later). While these developments are certainly important, the ratification and wide acceptance of 802.11b in late 1999 is widely regarded as the start of the popular wireless networking phenomenon.

It didn't take long for some sharp hacker types (and, indeed, a few CEO and FCC types) to realize that by using wireless client gear in conjunction with standard radio equipment, effective range can extend to more than 20 miles and potentially provide thousands of people with bandwidth reaching DSL speeds, for minimal hardware cost. Connectivity that previously had to creep up monopoly-held wires can now fly in through the walls with significantly higher performance. And since consumer-grade wireless equipment uses unlicensed radio spectrum, full-time connections can be set up *without paying a dime in airtime or licensing fees.*

While trumping the telco and cable companies with off-the-shelf magical hardware may be an entertaining fantasy, how well does wireless equipment designed to serve a few local clients actually perform in the real world? How can it be effectively applied to provide generalized access to the Internet?

The Problem

An obvious application for wireless is to provide the infamous "last mile" network service. This term refers to the stretch that sits between those who have good access to the Internet (ISPs, Telcos, and cable companies) and those who want it (consumers). This sort of arrangement requires wireless equipment at both ends of the stretch (for example, at an ISP's site and at a consumer's home).

Unfortunately, the nature of radio communications at microwave frequencies requires *line of sight* for optimal performance. This means that there should be an unobstructed view between the two antennas, preferably with nothing but a valley between them. This is absolutely critical in long-distance, low-power applications. Radio waves penetrate many common materials, but range is significantly reduced when going through anything but air. Although increasing transmission power can help get through trees and other obstructions, simply adding amplifiers isn't always an option, as the FCC imposes strict limits on power. (We will return to this subject in detail in Chapter 7.)

Speaking of amplifiers, a related technical obstacle to wireless nirvana is how to deal with noise in the band. The 2.4Ghz band isn't reserved for use solely by wireless networking gear. It has to share the band with many other devices, including cordless phones, wireless X-10 cameras, Bluetooth equipment, burglar alarms, and even microwave ovens! Using amplifiers to try to "blast" one's way through intervening obstacles and above the background noise is the social equivalent of turning your television up to full volume so you can hear it in your front yard (maybe also to hear it above your ringing telephone and barking dog, or maybe even your neighbor's loud television...).

If data is going to flow freely over the air, there has to be a high degree of coordination between those who set it up. As the airwaves are a public resource, the wireless infrastructure should be built in a way that benefits the most people possible, for the lowest cost. How can wireless networking effectively connect people to each other?

The WISP Approach

Visions of license-free, monopoly-shattering, high-bandwidth networks are certainly dancing through the heads of some business-minded individuals these days. On the surface, it looks like sound reasoning: if people are conditioned into believing that 6Mb DSL costs $250 per month to provide, then they'll certainly be willing to pay at least that much for an 11Mb wireless connection that costs pennies to operate, particularly if it's cleverly packaged as an upgrade to a brand name they already know. The temptation of high profits and low operating costs seems to have once again allowed marketing to give way to good sense. Thus, the "Wireless DSL" phenomenon was born. (Who needs an actual technology when you can market an acronym, anyway?)

In practice, many WISPs* are finding out that it's not as simple as throwing some antennas up and raking in the cash. To start with, true DSL provides a full-duplex, switched line. Most DSL lines are asymmetric, meaning that they allow for a higher download speed at the expense of slower upload speed. This difference is hardly noticeable when most of the network traffic is incoming (i.e., when users are browsing the web), but it is present. Even with the low-speed upload limitation, a full-duplex line can still upload and download data *simultaneously*. Would-be wireless providers that build on consumer-grade wireless technology are limited to half-duplex, shared bandwidth connections. That means that to actually provide the same quality of service as a wired DSL line, they would need four radios for each customer: two at each end, using one for upstream and one for downstream service. If the network infrastructure plan is to provide a few (or even a few dozen) wireless access sites throughout a city, these would need to be shared between all of the users, further degrading network performance, much like the cable modem nightmare. Additional access sites could help, but adding equipment also adds to hardware and operating costs.

Speaking of access points, where exactly should they be placed? Naturally, the antennas should be located wherever the greatest expected customer base can see them. Unless you've tried it, I guarantee this is trickier than it sounds. Trees, metal buildings, chain-link fences, and the natural lay of the land make antenna placement an interesting challenge for a hobbyist, but a nightmare for a network engineer. As we'll see later, an antenna site at least needs power and a sturdy mast to mount equipment on, and, preferably, it also has access to a wired backbone. Otherwise, even more radio gear is needed to provide network service to the tower.

Suppose that marketing has sufficiently duped would-be customers and claims to have enough tower sites to make offering network services at least a possibility. Now imagine that a prospective customer actually calls, requesting service. How does the WISP know if service is possible? With DSL, it's straightforward: look up the customer's phone number in the central database, figure out about how far they are from the CO, and give them an estimate. Unfortunately, no known database can tell you for certain what a given address has line of sight to.

---

* Wireless Internet Service Providers. No, I didn't make that one up.

As we'll see later, topographical software can help perform some preliminary work to help rule out the definite impossibilities. Some topographical packages even include tree and ground clutter data, although these tend to be considerably more expensive (and of dubious real value, unless they are up-to-date). Using such software, we might even be able to upgrade the potential customer to a "maybe." Ultimately, however, the only way to know if a particular customer can reach the WISP's backbone over wireless is to send out a tech with test gear, and try it.

So now the poor WISP must be prepared to "roll a truck" for new installations, making on-site calls to people who aren't even customers yet. If they're lucky, technicians might even get a test shot to work. At this point, finally, equipment can be installed, contracts signed, and the customer can get online at something almost resembling DSL. That is, be online until a bird perches on the antenna, or a new building goes up in the link path, or the leaves come out in the spring and block most of the signal (at which point, I imagine the customer would be referred to the fine print on that contract).

I think you can begin to see exactly where the bottom line is going in this sort of arrangement. The private WISP approach is filled with unanticipated (and expensive) challenges it comes to solving the problem of ubiquitous access on a large scale. What hope does our "wireless everywhere" vision have in light of all of the previously mentioned problems? Perhaps a massively parallel approach would help…

The Cooperative Approach

The difficulties of a commercial approach to wireless access exist because of a single social phenomenon: the customer is purchasing a solution and is therefore expecting a reasonable level of service for their money. In a commercial venture, the WISP is ultimately responsible for upholding their end of the agreement or otherwise compensating the customer.

The "last mile" problem has a very different outlook if each member of the network is responsible for keeping his own equipment online. Like many ideas whose time has come, the community access wireless network phenomenon is unfolding right now, all over the planet. People who are fed up with long lead times and high equipment and installation costs are pooling their resources to provide wireless access to friends, family, neighbors, schools, and remote areas that will likely never see broadband access otherwise. As difficult as the WISP nightmare example has made this idea sound, people everywhere are learning that they don't necessarily need to pay their dues to the telco to make astonishing things happen. They are discovering that it is indeed possible to provide very high bandwidth connections to those who need it for pennies—not hundreds of dollars—a month.

Of course, people who are expected to run a wireless gateway need access either to highly technical information, or to a solution that is no more difficult than plugging in a connector and flipping a switch. While bringing common experiences together can help find an easy solution more quickly, only a relatively small percentage of people on this planet know that microwave communications are even possible. Even fewer know how to effectively connect a wireless network to the Internet. As we'll see later, ubiquity is critical if wide area wireless access is going to be usable (even to the techno über-elite). It is in *everyone's* best interest to cooperate, share what they know, and help make bandwidth as pervasive as the air we breathe.

The desire to end this separation of "those in the know" from "those who want to know" is helping to bring people away from their computer screens and back into their local neighborhoods. In the last year, hundreds of independent local groups have formed with a very similar underlying principle: get people connected to each other for the lowest possible cost. Web sites, mailing lists, community meetings, and even IRC channels are being set up to share information about extending wireless network access to those who need it. Wherever possible, ingeniously simple and inexpensive (yet powerful) designs are being drawn up and given away. Thousands of people are working on this problem not for a personal profit motive, but for the benefit of the planet.

It is worth pointing out here that ISPs and telcos are in no way threatened by this technology; in fact, Internet service will be in even greater demand as wireless cooperatives come online. The difference is that many end users will have access without the need to tear down trees and dig up streets, and many others may find that network access in popular areas will be provided gratis, as a community service or on a cooperative trust basis, rather than as a corporate commodity.

Wireless networks can also be a tremendous boon in helping to fight censorship (both intentional and accidental). In traditional wired networks, those responsible for the existence of the network can exert a high degree of control over what happens "on their wires." Through border firewalls, proxies, packet filters, and clever routing, the ultimate network content that is available to an individual can be manipulated to an almost infinite degree. Even well-intentioned administrators who might block a port or service "for the good of the network" can unintentionally restrict the flow of information for perfectly legitimate users.

The rules are very different when the wires are taken away. Anyone with a wireless card can effectively generate whatever sort of packet they like and send it out to anyone within range. As long as nodes can agree on a common method of communications, any number of wireless networks can be created to exchange data in a way that makes it prohibitively difficult for a single entity to impose any sort of restriction on the flow of that data. Since the people involved in setting up such networks are by definition trying to communicate with each other, this can help bring about a strong sense of community. Many people find that they enjoy having a hand in building a communications infrastructure that fits their needs.

About This Book

The ultimate goal of this book is to get you excited about this technology, and arm you with the information you need to make it work in your community. We will demonstrate various techniques and equipment for connecting wireless networks to wired networks, and look at how others "in the know" are getting their neighborhoods, schools, and businesses talking to each other over the air. Along the way, we will visit the outer limits of what is possible with wireless networking, including how to stretch the range to miles and provide access for hundreds. If your budget won't allow for all of the networking gear you need, we'll show you how to build some of your own.

Through the efforts of countless volunteers and hobbyists, more bits are being moved more cheaply and easily than at any other time in history. There is more happening in the wireless world right now than is practical to put down on paper. Get online and find out what others in your area are doing with this technology (extensive online references are provided throughout, and in the Appendixes).

I hope you will find this book a useful and practical tool on your journey toward your own wireless utopia.

## CHAPTER 2

Defining Project Scope

*The nice thing about standards is that
there are so many to choose from.*
—Andrew S. Tanenbaum, c.1980

What do you want to accomplish? As a system administrator, this is a question I ask whenever a user comes to me with a new request. It's easy to get wrapped up in implementation details while forgetting exactly what it is you set out to do in the first place. As projects get more complex, it's easy to find yourself "spinning your wheels" without actually getting anywhere.

The most common questions I've encountered about wireless networking seem to be the simplest:

- What is the difference between 802.11a/b/g, 802.16, and 802.1x?
- How much does it cost?
- How far will it go?
- Can I use it to do [fill in the blank]?

The first question is by far the most straightforward to answer—the rest all depend on your application and circumstances. Before we can start building networks, we need to have a clear idea of what we have to work with.

The Standards

Here's a brief overview of the current (and future) standards that all fall under the 802 family:

802.11

The first wireless standard to be defined in the 802 family was 802.11. It was approved by the IEEE in 1997, and defines three possible physical layers: FHSS at 2.4GHz, DSSS at 2.4GHz, and Infrared. 802.11 could achieve data rates of 1 or 2Mbps. 802.11 radios that use DSSS are interoperable with 802.11b and 802.11g radios at those speeds, while FHSS radios and Infrared are obviously not.

802.11a

According to the specifications available from the IEEE (*http://standards. ieee.org/getieee802/*), both 802.11a and 802.11b were ratified on September 16, 1999. Early on, 802.11a was widely touted as the "802.11b killer," as it not only provides significantly faster data rates (up to 54Mbps), but operates in a completely different spectrum, the 5GHz UNII band. It uses an encoding technique called Orthogonal Frequency Division Multiplexing (OFDM). While the promise of higher speeds and freedom from interference with 2.4GHz devices made 802.11a sound promising, it came to market much later than 802.11b. 802.11a also suffers from range problems: at the same power and gain, signals at 5GHz appear to travel only half as far as signals at 2.4GHz, presenting a real technical hurdle for designers and implementers. The rapid adoption of 802.11b only made matters worse, since users of 802.11b gear didn't have a clear upgrade path to 802.11a (the two are incompatible). As a result, 802.11a isn't nearly as ubiquitous or inexpensive as 802.11b, although client cards and dual-band access points (which essentially incorporate two radios, or a single radio with a dual-band chipset) are coming down in price.

802.11b

Throughout this book, I mainly discuss 802.11b. It is the de facto wireless networking standard of the last few years, and for good reason. It offers excellent range and respectable throughput (while the radio can send frames at up to 11Mbps, protocol overhead puts the data rate at 5 to 6Mbps, on par with 10baseT wired Ethernet). It operates using DSSS at 2.4GHz, and will automatically select the best data rate (1, 2, 5.5, or 11Mbps), depending on available signal strength. Its greatest advantage at this point is its ubiquity: millions of 802.11b devices have shipped, and the cost of client and access point gear is not only phenomenally low, but many laptop and handheld devices now ship with 802.11b connectivity. Since it can move data at rates much faster than the average Internet connection, 802.11b is widely regarded as "good enough" for general use.

802.11g

While the 802.11g specification hasn't yet been ratified by the IEEE, it will likely be passed by the time this book goes to press. 802.11g uses the OFDM encoding of 802.11a in the 2.4GHz band, and will also fall back to DSSS to maintain backward compatibility with 802.11b radios. This means that speeds of 54Mbps are theoretically achievable in the 2.4GHz band, all while keeping backwards compatibility with existing 802.11b gear. This is a very promising technology (so promising, in fact, that the lack of ratification hasn't stopped some manufacturers from shipping gear that uses the draft standard). In all likelihood, equipment that ships now will be upgradeable to 802.11g via a firmware update once the actual specification is ratified. 802.11g will likely be a massively popular technology; it promises many of the advantages of 802.11a without significantly greater cost while maintaining backward compatibility. For these reasons, 802.11g is poised to become the next major ubiquitous wireless technology.

802.16

Approved on December 6, 2001, 802.16 promises to overcome all of the shortcomings of long-distance applications encountered by people using 802.11 protocols. It should be pointed out that the 802.11 family was never intended to provide long-distance, metropolitan-area coverage (although I'll show you some examples of people doing exactly that). The 802.16 specification is specifically designed for providing wireless infrastructure that will cover entire cities, with typical ranges measured in kilometers. It will use frequencies from 10 to 66GHz to provide commercial-quality services to stationary locations (i.e., buildings). As I write this, a new extension that will operate in the 2 to 11GHz range (802.16a) has just been ratified. This should help significantly with the line-of-sight problems posed by the extremely short waves of 10 to 66GHz. Equipment that implements 802.16 is just now coming to market, and will likely be priced well above the consumer-grade equipment of the 802.11 family.

802.1x

The 802.1x protocol is not actually a wireless protocol. It describes a method for port authentication that can be applied to nearly any network connection, wired or wireless. Chapter 3 covers 802.1x in more detail.

At this point, the clear front-runner in wireless technology is 802.11b, so I will focus on it for the remainder of this book. Of course, this state of affairs will change as time goes on and consumer demands bring new products to market. For a good overview of 802.11 technologies (including a bunch that I don't have space to cover here), take a look at *http://www.80211-planet.com/tutorials/article.php/1439551*. You can also download the specifications from the IEEE for yourself at *http://standards.ieee.org/getieee802/*.

Our original questions (how much does 802.11b cost, how far it will go, and what it is good for) all have the same practical answer: "It depends!" It is easiest to explain how people have applied wireless to fit their needs and answer these questions by way of example.

People are using wireless networking in three general applications: *point-to-point links*, *point-to-multipoint links*, and *ad-hoc* (or *peer-to-peer*) *workgroups*. A typical point-to-point application would be to provide network bandwidth where there isn't any otherwise available. For example, suppose you have a DSL line at your office, but can't get one installed at your house (due to CO distance limits). If you have an unobstructed view of your home from your office, you can probably set up a point-to-point connection to connect the two together. With proper antennas and clear line of sight, reliable point-to-point links in excess of 20 miles are possible.

One common way of using wireless in a point-to-multipoint application is to set up an access point at home to let several laptop users simultaneously browse the Internet from wherever they happen to be (the living room couch is a typical example). Whenever several nodes are talking to a single, central point of access, this is a *point-to-multipoint* application. But point-to-multipoint doesn't have to end at home. Suppose you work for a school that has a fast Internet connection run to one building, but other buildings on your campus aren't wired together. You could use an access point in the wired building with a single antenna that all of the other buildings can see. This would allow the entire campus to share the Internet bandwidth for a fraction of the cost of wiring, in a matter of days rather than months.

The last class of networking, ad-hoc (or peer-to-peer) applies whenever an access point isn't available. In peer-to-peer mode, nodes with the same network settings can talk to each other, as long as they are within range. The big benefit of this mode of operations is that even if none of the nodes are in range of a central access point, they can still talk to each other. This is ideal for quickly transferring files between your laptop and a friend's when you are out of range of an access point, for example. In addition, if one of the nodes in range happens to be an Internet gateway, traffic can be relayed to and from the Internet, just as if it were a conventional access point. In Chapter 5, we'll see a method for using this mode to provide gateway services without the need for a hardware access point. In Chapter 7, we'll build on that simple gateway to create a public access wireless gatekeeper, with dynamic firewalling, a captive web portal, user authentication, and real-time traffic shaping.

You can use these modes of operation in conjunction with each other (and with other wired networking techniques) to extend your network as you need it. It is common, for example, to use a long-distance wireless link to provide access to a remote location, and then set up an access point at that end to provide local access. Multiple point-to-point links can also be linked together to create a large network that extends many miles beyond the area of readily available broadband Internet access.

Hardware Requirements

The total cost of your project is largely dependent on your project goals and how much work you're willing to do for yourself. While you can certainly spend tens of thousands on outdoor, ISP-class equipment, you may find that you can save money (and get more satisfaction) building similar functionality yourself, from cheaper off-the-shelf hardware.

If you simply want to connect your laptop to someone else's 802.11b network, you'll need only a client card and driver software (at this point, compatible cards cost between $30 and $100). Like most equipment, the price typically goes up with added features, such as an external antenna connector, higher output power, a more sensitive radio, and the usual bells and whistles. Once you select a card, find out what the network settings are for the network you want to connect to and hop on. If you need more range, a small omnidirectional antenna (typically $50–$100) can significantly extend the roaming range of your laptop.

If you want to provide wireless network access to other people, you'll need an access point (AP). This has become something of a loaded term, and can refer to anything from a low-end "residential gateway" class box (about $100) to high-end, commercial quality, multi-radio equipment ($1000+). They are typically small, standalone boxes that contain at least one radio and another network connection (such as Ethernet or a dialup modem). For the rest of this book, we'll use the term "access point" (or the acronym AP) to refer to any device capable of providing network access to your wireless clients. As we'll see in Chapter 5, this can even be provided by a conventional PC router equipped with a wireless card.

While a radio and an access point can provide a simple short-range network, you will more than likely want to extend your coverage beyond what is possible out of the box. The most effective way of extending range is to use external antennas. Antennas come in a huge assortment of packages, from small omnidirectional tabletop antennas to large, mast-mounted parabolic dishes. There isn't one "right" antenna for every application; you'll need to choose the antenna that fits your needs (if you're trying to cover just a single building, you may not even need external antennas). Take a look at Chapter 6 for specific antenna descriptions.

Draw a Picture

Before you price a single piece of network equipment or visit a site, try to get an idea of exactly what you want to accomplish. Are you trying to add wireless access to a house that already has a cable modem connection to the

Internet? Do you want to share a commercial DSL line with a neighbor across the street? Are you trying to connect several campus buildings together that already have an internal wired infrastructure?

It can be very helpful to draw an overview picture of your project before you worry about too many technical details. You can use programs such as Visio, XFig, or OmniGraffle to help you create a simple network diagram quickly, then fill in actual details as you accumulate them. How far apart are the potential sites? What sort of coverage do you need? Where does the Internet fit into the picture? Are there any obstacles in the path? How many apparent obstacles can be turned to your advantage? Remember that you can turn many hills that are "in the path" into high repeater sites with a bit of effort.

Once you have determined your goals, you can visit actual sites and start looking for the required gear.

Site Survey

The most efficient wireless network consists of a single client talking to a single access point a few feet away with an absolutely clear line of sight between them and no other noise on the channel being used (either from other networks or from equipment that shares the 2.4GHz spectrum). Of course, with the possible exception of the home wireless LAN, these ideal conditions simply aren't feasible. All of your users will need to "share the airwaves," and it's more than likely that they won't be able to see the access point from where they are located. Fortunately, 802.11b gear is very tolerant of less than optimal conditions at close range. When planning your network, be sure to look out for the following:

- Objects that absorb microwave signals, such as trees, earth, brick, plaster walls, and people
- Objects that reflect or diffuse signals, such as metal, fences, tinted windows, mylar, pipes, screens, and bodies of water
- Sources of 2.4GHz noise, such as microwave ovens, cordless phones, wireless X-10 cameras and automation equipment, and other 802.11b networks

The more you can eliminate from the path between your access points and your clients, the happier you'll be. You won't be able to get rid of every obstacle, but you should be able to minimize their impact by working around them.

You may have total control over your own access points and other 2.4GHz equipment, but what about your neighbors? How can you tell what channels are in use in your local area?

While a spectrum analyzer (and an engineer to run it) is the ultimate survey tool, such things don't come cheap. Fortunately, you can get a lot of useful information using a good quality client radio and software. Take a look at the tools that come with your wireless gear. Lucent's Site Monitor tool (shown in Figure 2-1), which ships with Orinoco/Agere/Avaya/Proxim cards, is particularly handy. You should be able to get an overview map of all networks in range, and which channels they're using.

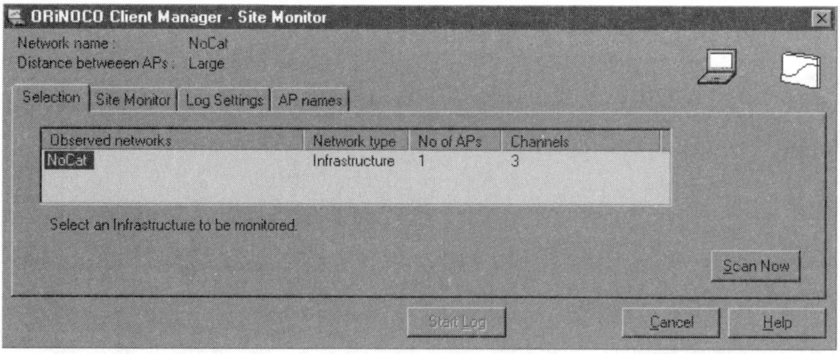

Figure 2-1. Lucent's Site Monitor tool shows who's using 802.11b in your area

A good client monitoring tool should get you started with simple surveying, but may not give you all the detail you need. See Chapter 7 for more tools that can show you exactly who's doing what on the airwaves in your area.

Other (non-802.11b) sources of 2.4GHz radio emissions show up as noise on your signal strength meter. If you encounter a lot of noise on the channel you'd like to use, you can try to minimize it by moving your access point, using a more directional antenna (see Chapter 6), or simply picking a different channel. While you always want to maximize your received signal, it is usable only if the ambient noise is low. The relationship of signal to noise is critical for any kind of communications. It is frequently abbreviated as SNR, for signal to noise ratio. As this number increases, so does the likelihood that you'll have reliable communications.

802.11b Channels and Interference

The IEEE 802.11b specification details 11 possible overlapping frequencies[*] on which communications can take place. Much like the different channels

---

[*] In the U.S., anyway. Canadian radios can go up to channel 13, and Japanese radios operate only on channel 14. For the full international frequency channel plan, see Table 105 of the IEEE 802.11b-1999 specification at *http://standards.ieee.org/getieee802*.

on a cordless phone, changing the channel can help eliminate noise that degrades network performance and can even allow multiple networks to coexist in the same physical space without interfering with each other.

Rather than attempting to set up a single central access point with a high-gain omnidirectional antenna, you will probably find it more effective to set up several low-range, overlapping cells. If you use access point hardware, and all of the APs are connected to the same physical network segment, users can even roam seamlessly between cells.

This spectrum's 11 overlapping channels are shown in Table 2-1.

Table 2-1. 802.11b channel frequencies

Channel	Center frequency (GHz)
1	2.412
2	2.417
3	2.422
4	2.427
5	2.432
6	2.437
7	2.442
8	2.447
9	2.452
10	2.457
11	2.462

The channels actually use 22MHz of signal bandwidth, so adjacent radios will need to be separated by at least five channels to see zero overlap. For example, channels 1, 6, and 11 have no overlap. Neither do 2 and 7, 3 and 8, 4 and 9, or 5 and 10. While you will ideally want to use non-overlapping channels for your access points, in a crowded setting (such as a city apartment building or office park) this is becoming less of an option. It is possible, although not ideal, to use channels that are closer together. For example, you can use channels 1 and 4 in the same space.

You stand a better chance at saturating your area with usable signal from many low-power cells rather than a single tower with a high-gain antenna. As your individual cells won't need a tremendous range to cover a wide area, you can use lower gain (and lower cost) antennas, further limiting the chances of interfering with other gear in the band. As you can see in Figure 2-2, you could use as few as three channels to cover an infinitely large area, with no channel overlap whatsoever.

Figure 2-2. Using non-adjacent channels, several APs can cover a large area

The worst possible case would involve two separate, busy networks trying to occupy the same channel, right next to each other. The further you can get away from this nightmare of collisions, the better. Realistically, a single channel can easily support 50 or more simultaneous users, and a fair amount of channel overlap is tolerable. The radios use the air only when they actually have something to transmit, and retransmit automatically on error, so heavy congestion feels more or less like ordinary net lag to the end user. The sporadic nature of most network traffic helps to share the air and avoid collisions, like playing cards shuffling together into a pack.

To sum up: be a good neighbor, and think about what you're doing before turning on your own gear. The radio spectrum is a public resource and, with a little bit of cooperation, can be used by everyone to gain greater access to network resources.

Topographical Mapping 101

As you roll out wireless equipment, you'll find yourself looking at your environment in a different way. Air conditioning ducts, pipes, microwave ovens, power lines, and other sources of nastiness start leaping into the foreground as you walk around. By the time you've set up a couple of nodes, you will most likely be familiar with every source of noise or reflection in the area you're trying to cover. But what if you want to extend your range, as in a several mile point-to-point link? Is there a better way to survey the outlying environment other than walking the entire route of your link? Maybe.

Topographical surveys have been made (and are constantly being revised) by the USGS in every region of the United States. Topo (short for topographical) maps are available on both paper and CD-ROM from a variety of sources. If you want to know how the land lies between two points, the USGS topos are a good starting point.

The paper topo maps are a great resource for getting an overview of the surrounding terrain in your local area. You can use a ruler to quickly gauge the approximate distance between two points, and to determine whether there are any obvious obstructions in the path. While they're a great place to start assessing a long link, topographical maps don't provide some critical information: namely, tree and building data. The land may appear to cooperate on paper, but if there's a forest or several tall buildings between your two points, there's not much hope for a direct shot.

The USGS also provides DOQs (or Digital Orthophoto Quadrangles) of actual aerial photography. Unfortunately, freely available versions of DOQs tend to be out of date (frequently 8 to 10 years old), and recent DOQs are not only expensive but often aren't even available. If you absolutely must have the latest aerial photographs of your local area, the USGS will let you download them for $30 per order and $7.50–$15 per file. You will probably find it cheaper and easier to make an initial estimate with topo maps and then simply go out and try the link.

Interestingly enough, MapQuest (*http://www.mapquest.com/*) has recently started providing color aerial photos (in addition to their regular street maps) from GlobeXplorer (*http://www.globexplorer.com/*). While there's little indication as to how recent their data is, it may be a good place to get a quick (and free) aerial overview of your local area. Another popular software package is EarthViewer3D by Keyhole Software (*http://www.earthviewer.com/*). It incorporates satellite image data, aerial photography, GIS data, and business databases into an interactive overview map.

You can buy paper maps from most camping supply stores, or browse them online for free at *http://www.topozone.com/*. If you're interested in DOQs, go to the USGS directly at *http://earthexplorer.usgs.gov/*. We'll take a look at some nifty things you can do with topo maps on CD-ROM and your GPS in Chapter 6.

## CHAPTER 3

Network Layout

*A common mistake that people
make when trying to design something
completely foolproof is to underestimate
the ingenuity of complete fools.*
—Douglas Adams

As we saw in Chapter 2, there is an astounding variety of wireless networking equipment available on the consumer market today. While the champion technology of wireless community networks is still 802.11b, simply choosing equipment that is "Wi-Fi" compliant won't necessarily guarantee a successful network project.

While equipment features, capabilities, and prices tend to change drastically in a short time, the essential network functions that they perform are still very straightforward. Let's look at what your devices need to provide in order to fulfill your wireless networking dreams.

Layer 1 (Physical) Connectivity

Before any two components of your network can talk to each other, they must share a common physical medium through which they communicate. In the wired world, this is obvious; you would never try to connect a copper CAT5 cable to a piece of fiber and expect it all to "just work."

In the wireless world, every device from your network to your cordless phone to your garage door opener must share the same physical medium: electromagnetic waves radiating through the air. It is possible for all of these devices to communicate without interfering with each other because they can be made sensitive to a particular portion of the vast electromagnetic spectrum. This is analogous to tuning channels on a radio or TV—many channels are broadcasting simultaneously, but they are well-coordinated and only use a portion of the available spectrum, to avoid interfering with each other.

So before any other considerations, devices that need to intercommunicate on your network must be able to send signals in the same frequency range. Obviously, an 802.11b card operating at 2.4GHz doesn't have a chance of carrying on a conversation with an 802.11a Access Point speaking at 5GHz. In addition to using a particular frequency range, each wireless protocol also defines a plan for using that range. For example, the original 802.11 specification defines two RF modulation schemes, FHSS and DSSS. Both operate at 2.4GHz, but use the spectrum differently. Frequency Hopping Spread Spectrum (FHSS) breaks the available spectrum into 77 channels, each 1MHz wide. It uses a time-based, pseudo-random algorithm to quickly skip between all of the available channels in an attempt to avoid noise from other 2.4GHz devices. As we saw in Chapter 2, Direct Sequence Spread Spectrum (DSSS) breaks the same frequency range into 11 overlapping channels, each 5MHz apart (but 22MHz wide). It uses one channel at a time and employs more sophisticated encoding techniques to avoid noise and increase the data rate. Although FHSS and DSSS devices both operate "at 2.4GHz," they have no hope of being able to communicate with each other.

Whatever wireless equipment you choose, be sure that both ends are capable of speaking the same protocol at the same frequency range, whether that's 802.11b speaking DSSS at 2.4GHz, 802.11a speaking OFDM at 5GHz, 802.11g speaking OFDM at 2.4GHz, or something altogether different, new, and wonderful. If two pieces of equipment claim compatibility with the same IEEE standard (such as 802.11b), they should theoretically be able to interoperate. Be sure to check the fine print on any device that only claims compatibility with an umbrella term (such as Wi-Fi), because the definition of the term can change at the whims of marketing moguls.*

As 802.11b is by far the most common technology used in the wireless community effort, we will focus on its particulars for the rest of this chapter.

Layer "1.5" Connectivity

Simply using equipment that adheres to the same standard on the same channel doesn't quite fulfill the requirements of Layer 1 (physical) connectivity. There are a few more protocol requirements that must be met before we can move on to Layer 2.

802.11b defines two possible (and mutually exclusive) radio modes that stations can use to intercommunicate. Those modes are *BSS* and *IBSS*.

---

* At the time of this writing, the term Wi-Fi can refer to either 802.11b or 802.11a gear, which are *not* interoperable. Wi-Fi5 was supposed to refer to 5GHz gear, but evidently that didn't fly. For a good laugh, see *http://news.com.com/2100-1033-960880.html*.

BSS stands for Basic Service Set. In this operating mode, one station (the *BSS master*, usually a piece of hardware called an access point, or AP) provides wireless-to-Ethernet bridging. Before gaining access to the wired network, wireless clients (also called *BSS clients*) must first establish communications with an access point within range, as shown in Figure 3-1. Once the AP has authenticated the wireless client, it allows packets to flow between the client and the attached wired network, either routing traffic at Layer 3, or acting as a true Layer 2 bridge. A related term, Extended Service Set (ESS), refers to a physical subnet that contains more than one AP. In this sort of arrangement, the APs can communicate with each other to allow authenticated clients to "roam" between them, handing off IP information as the clients move about. Note that (as of this writing) there are no APs that allow roaming across networks separated by a router.*

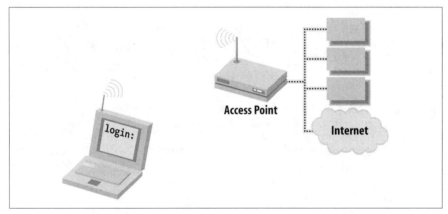

Figure 3-1. In BSS (or ESS) mode, clients must associate with an AP before accessing the wired network

IBSS stands for Independent Basic Service Set, and is frequently referred to as ad-hoc or peer-to-peer mode. In this mode, no hardware AP is required. Any network node that is within range of any other can communicate if both nodes agree on a few basic parameters. If one of those peers also has a wired connection to another network, it can provide access to that network. Figure 3-2 shows a model of an IBSS network.

Note that an 802.11b radio must be set to work in either of these modes, but cannot work in both simultaneously. Both modes support shared-key WEP encryption (more on that later).

---

* This is a difficult problem that experimental technologies such as Mobile IP attempt to solve.

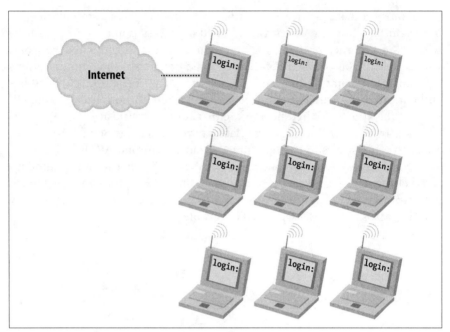

Figure 3-2. In IBSS mode, nodes can talk to any other node within range; a node with another network connection can provide gateway services

I give specific examples of how to set up BSS and IBSS networks in Chapters 4 and 5. Once you have two or more IBSS mode stations, or a BSS master and one or more BSS clients all within range, you are ready to move on to actual networking.

Layer 2 and Up

Once the physical layer is established, a wireless network is very much like a traditional Ethernet network. Assuming that you want to connect your wireless clients to the Internet, you'll want to provide all of the usual TCP/IP services that make networking so much fun (such as DNS and DHCP). To the rest of your network, wireless clients look like just another Ethernet interface, and are treated no differently than the wired printer down the hall. You can route, rewrite, tunnel, fold, spindle, and/or mutilate packets from your wireless clients just as you can with any other network device. Once wireless packets hit the wire, you use the same hubs, switches, and routers that make up the majority of traditional wired networks.

Wired Wireless

Presumably, no matter how many wireless clients you intend to support, you will eventually need to "hit the wire" in order to access other networks (such as the Internet). There are a number of different kinds of physical devices you can use to jump from wireless back to your wired infrastructure.

Access Point Hardware

APs are widely considered ideal for "campus" coverage. They provide a point of entry to the wired infrastructure that can be configured by a central authority. They typically allow for one or two radios per AP, theoretically supporting hundreds of simultaneous wireless users at a time. They must be configured with an ESSID (Extended Service Set ID, also known as the Network Name or WLAN Service Area ID, depending on who you talk to); it's a simple string that identifies the wireless network. Many APs use a client program for configuration and a simple password to protect their network settings. All hardware access points provide BSS master services.

Most APs also provide a number of enhanced features. External antennas (or antenna connectors), advanced link status monitoring, and extensive logging and statistics are now common on many APs. In addition, most access points provide two additional security measures: MAC address filtering and closed networks. With MAC filtering enabled, a client radio attempting access must have its MAC address listed on an internal table before it can associate with the AP. In a closed network, the AP doesn't beacon its ESSID at regular intervals. This means that each client must know the ESSID ahead of time, which makes it more difficult for people using programs such as *NetStumbler* to detect the network.

Other enhanced modes include dynamic WEP key management, public encryption key exchange, channel bonding, and other fun toys. Unfortunately, these extended modes are entirely manufacturer- (and model-) specific, are not covered by any established standard, and do not interoperate with other manufacturers' equipment.

In addition to dedicated AP hardware, certain radio cards (in particular, those based on the Prism 2 chipset) can be made to operate as a BSS master and act as if it were a regular AP. In Chapter 5, I will show you how to "roll your own" AP using the Host AP driver for Linux.

APs are by far the most widely used devices for providing wireless services, particularly in corporate networks. They provide a high degree of control over who can access the wire, but they are not cheap (the average AP at the time of this writing costs between $500 and $1000).

Another class of AP is occasionally referred to as a *residential gateway* (RG). The Apple Airport, Orinoco RG series, and Linksys WAP11 are popular examples of RGs. They are typically much less expensive than their "commercial" counterparts, costing between $100 and $300. Many have built-in modems, allowing for wireless-to-dialup access (which can be very handy, if Ethernet access isn't available). Most even provide Network Address Translation (NAT), DHCP, and bridging services for wireless clients. While they may not support as many simultaneous clients as a high-end AP, they can provide cheap, simple access for many applications. When configuring an inexpensive AP for bridged Ethernet mode, you can still have a high degree of control over what individual clients can access on the wired network by controlling communications at a higher level. See the "Captive Portal" discussion in Chapter 7 for more details.

Note that APs (that is, BSS masters) do *not* talk to each other over the air. In order to have 802.11b BSS mode communications, one device (e.g., an access point) must be a master, and the other must be a client.

BSS Client Hardware

While the typical BSS client is a PCMCIA or other plug-in radio card, there are also other hardware devices that will serve as a BSS client that connect directly to Ethernet. The Linksys WET11, 3Com Wireless Workgroup Bridge, and Orinoco Ethernet Converter are examples of this type of hardware. Some RGs (such as the Linksys WAP11) can even be made to operate as a BSS client. The typical *wireless client bridge* is a small box that provides one or more Ethernet ports and bridges them (at Layer 2) directly to a wireless network. The radio is configured via Ethernet (or a USB port) to act as a client to an existing wireless network. After initial configuration, no further interaction with the bridge is necessary. As far as the wired device is concerned, it is directly attached to an Ethernet network and requires no special drivers or other preparation to use the wireless network.

These devices are very handy in some circumstances, especially when you would like to get an Ethernet-equipped device onto the wireless network, but can't install a wireless card. One typical use is to connect an Ethernet printer to a wireless network, so you can install it somewhere that doesn't have CAT5 available. Another popular use for the WET11 is to bridge a console game (such as Sony PlayStation 2) to your wireless network, thereby avoiding the need to run CAT5 to your television. They are also handy for connecting remote access points back to a central wireless infrastructure. I'll provide an example of how to do that in Chapter 7.

The two big drawbacks to most BSS client hardware are price and performance. Since they aren't as popular as client cards, they are typically a bit more expensive. They are also tend to offer poor performance compared to client cards (2 to 4Mbps throughput is typical, compared to 5 to 6Mbps with client cards). Despite these issues, Ethernet bridges are an ideal solution to some networking problems.

Peer-to-Peer (IBSS) Networking

Radios that are operating in IBSS mode can communicate with each other without a hardware access point if they have the same ESSID and WEP settings. This is particularly handy for setting up temporary wireless workgroups without an AP, or for building point-to-point wireless connections. As stated earlier, any computer with an 802.11b card and another network connection (usually Ethernet, dialup, or even another wireless connection) can serve as a gateway between the two networks.

There is one important constraint on using IBSS mode: although it is defined by the 802.11b standard, few client cards actually interoperate well in the real world with others using IBSS. While two radios of the same manufacturer (and of the same firmware revision) generally work just fine, trying to get a Cisco card to talk to a Proxim card in IBSS mode (for example) is usually futile.

With this in mind, why would you choose to use IBSS mode rather than use an AP or the Host AP driver? There are a couple of reasons. If you happen to have two cards of the same manufacturer and a couple of old computers, IBSS mode is ideal if you want to create a fixed point-to-point connection. Also, Host AP supports only a limited set of wireless cards—if you already own a card that isn't supported, you're out of luck. Finally, if you're using a laptop and need to exchange data with another wireless user, IBSS is your only option if you're out of range of an AP and can't run Host AP.

In Chapter 5, I'll build a Linux-based wireless gateway from scratch, using both IBSS mode and the Host AP driver. In Chapter 7, I'll examine one method of extending the gateway to provide different classes of service, depending on who connects to it.

Vital Services

A network can be as simple as a PPP dialup to an ISP, or as grandiose and baroque as a multinational corporate MegaNet. But every node on a multi-million dollar network in Silicon Valley needs to address the same fundamental questions that a dialup computer must answer: *who am I, where am I going,* and *how do I get there from here?* In order for wireless clients to easily access a network, the following basic services must be provided.

DHCP

The days of static IP addresses and user-specified network parameters are thankfully far behind us. Using DHCP (Dynamic Host Configuration Protocol),* it is possible (and even trivial) to set up a server that responds to client requests for network information. Typically, a DHCP server provides all of the information that a client needs to begin routing packets on the network, including the client's own IP address, the default Internet gateway, and the IP addresses of the local DNS servers. The client configuration is ridiculously easy and is, in fact, configured out of the box for DHCP in all modern operating systems.

While a thorough dissection of DHCP is beyond the scope of this book, a typical DHCP session goes something like this: a client boots up, knowing nothing about the network it is attached to except its own hardware MAC address. It broadcasts a packet saying effectively, "I am here, and this is my MAC address. What is my IP address?" A DHCP server on the same network segment is listening for these requests, and responds with "Hello MAC address, here is your IP address, and by the way here is the IP address to route outgoing packets to, and some DNS servers are over there. Come back in a little while and I'll give you more information." The client, now armed with a little bit of knowledge, goes about its merry way. Figure 3-3 shows how this conversation takes place.

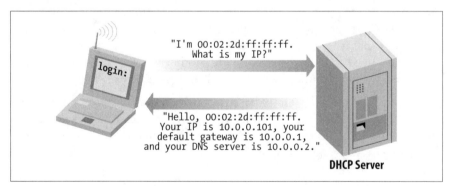

Figure 3-3. DHCP lets a node get its network settings dynamically and easily

---

* See *http://rfc.net/rfc1533.html* for an overview.

In a wireless environment, DHCP is an absolute necessity. There isn't much point in being able to wander around without a cable if you need to manually set the network parameters for whatever network you happen to be in range of. It's much more convenient to let the computers work it out on their own (and let you get back to more important things, such as IRC or "Quake III Arena"). Since DHCP lets a node discover information about its network, it's easy to get "online" without any prior knowledge about that particular network's layout. This service demonstrates a condition that network administrators have known for years: users just want to get online without knowing (or even caring) about the underlying network. From their perspective, it should just work. DHCP makes this kind of magic possible.

From a network administrator's perspective, the magic isn't terribly difficult to bring about. As long as you have exactly one DHCP server running on your network segment, your clients can all pull from a pool of available IP addresses. The DHCP server will manage the pool on its own, reclaiming addresses that are no longer in use and reassigning them to new clients.

In many cases, a wired network's existing DHCP server serves wireless users with no trouble. It will see the wireless node's DHCP request just as it would any other and responds accordingly. If your wired network isn't already providing DHCP, or if your access point isn't capable of Layer 2 bridging, then the access point itself will likely provide DHCP. I'll cover setting up DHCP services on a homebrew wireless gateway in more detail in Chapter 5.

DNS

My, how different the online world would be if we talked about sending mail to *rob@208.201.239.36*, or got excited about having just been *64.28.67.150*'d. DNS is the dynamic telephone directory of the Internet, mapping human friendly names (such as *oreillynet.com* or *slashdot.org*) to computer friendly numbers (such as the dotted quads mentioned previously). The Internet without DNS is about as much fun and convenient as referring to people by their Social Security Numbers.

Much like DHCP, your network's existing DNS servers should be more than adequate to provide name resolution services to your wireless clients. However, depending on your particular wireless application, you may want to get creative with providing additional DNS services. A caching DNS server might be appropriate, to reduce the load on your primary DNS servers (especially if you have a large number of wireless clients). You might even want to run dynamic DNS for your wireless hosts, so that wireless nodes can easily provide services for each other.

One handy use for DNS is to provide local top-level domains (TLDs) that don't normally resolve on the Internet, but direct people to local services. For example, the ad-hoc TLD of the NoCat network in Sebastopol is *.cat*, and the TLD for SeattleWireless is *.swn*. This allows for nifty names such as *gateway.rob.cat* or *music.nodeone.swn*. These addresses are not reachable by the Internet, but will resolve for anyone connected to the wireless network. I'll look at how various community network groups are extending TLD name service (and even connecting their networking projects via Internet tunnels) in Chapter 7.

NAT

In order for any machine to be reachable via the Internet, it must be possible to route traffic to it. A central authority, the IANA (Internet Assigned Numbers Authority, *http://www.iana.org*), holds the keys to the Internet. This international body controls how IP addresses are partitioned out to the various parts of the world, in an effort to keep every part of the Internet (theoretically) reachable from every other and to prevent the accidental reuse of IP addresses in different parts of the world. Unfortunately, due to the unexpected popularity of the Net, what was thought to be plenty of address space at design time has proven to be woefully inadequate in the real world. With thousands of new users coming online for the first time every day (and some large corporate users simply refusing to give up huge chunks of unused address space), the general consensus is that there simply aren't enough IP addresses to go around anymore. Most ISPs are increasingly paranoid about the shortage of homesteading space, and are loath to give out more than one per customer (and in many cases, they won't even do that anymore, thanks to the wonders of DHCP).

Now we see the inevitable problem: suppose you have a single IP address allocated to you by your ISP, but you want to allow Internet access to a bunch of machines, including your wireless nodes. You certainly don't want to pay exorbitant fees for more address space just to let your nephew get online when he brings his wireless laptop over once a month.

This is where NAT can help you. Truly a mixed blessing, NAT (referred to in some circles as "masquerading") provides a two-way forwarding service between the Internet and another network of computers. A computer providing NAT typically has two network interfaces. One interface is connected to the Internet (where it uses a real live IP address), and the other is attached to an internal network. Machines on the internal network use any of IANA's reserved IP addresses and route all of their outgoing traffic through the NAT box. When the NAT box receives a packet bound for the

Internet, it makes a note of where the packet came from. It then rewrites the packet using its "real" IP address, and sends the modified packet out to your ISP (where it winds its way through the rest of the Internet, hopefully arriving at the requested destination). When the response (if any) comes back, the NAT box looks up who made the original request, rewrites the inbound packet, and returns it to the original sender. As far as the rest of the Net is concerned, only the NAT machine is visible. And as far as the internal clients can tell, they're directly connected to the Internet. Figure 3-4 shows a NAT configuration.

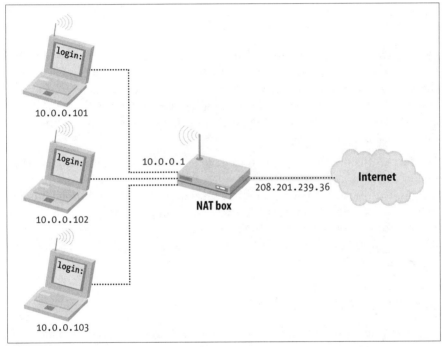

Figure 3-4. Using NAT, several computers can share a single "real" IP address

The IANA has reserved the following sets of IP addresses for private use (as outlined in RFC 1918, http://rfc.net/rfc1918.html):

```
10.0.0.0 to 10.255.255.255
172.16.0.0 to 172.31.255.255
192.168.0.0 to 192.168.255.255
```

These addresses will never be used on the Internet. As long as your internal machines use IP addresses in any of these three ranges, your traffic will not interfere with any other host on the Net.

NAT is handy, but isn't without its drawbacks. For example, some services may not work properly with some implementations of NAT. Most notably, active FTP sessions and some online games fail when running behind many NAT boxes. Another big disadvantage to NAT is that it effectively makes the Internet a read-only medium, much like television. If you can have only outbound traffic (to web servers, for example) but traffic from the Internet can't reach your machine directly, then you have no way of serving data and contributing back to the Net! This doesn't prevent you from using two-way services such as IRC and email, but it does preclude you from easily running on-demand services where Internet users connect to you directly (for example, running your own web server from behind a NAT isn't trivial, unless you're the one who controls the NAT).

Despite these drawbacks, NAT is an invaluable tool for allowing throngs of people to access Internet resources. In Chapter 5, I'll build a Linux gateway that will do NAT for you and handle almost every popular form of Internet traffic you care to throw at it (including active FTP). In Chapter 7, I will extend it even further, to try to get around some of the potentially antisocial aspects of NAT.

Of course, if you're lucky enough to have a ton of live IP address space, feel free to flaunt it and assign live IPs to your wireless clients! Naturally, most people (and, indeed, their laptops) are unprepared for the unbridled adrenal rush of using a live IP address without a firewall. But if you have that many real IPs to throw around, you must be used to living large. Just don't worry when you find your clients spontaneously rebooting or suddenly serving 0-dAy W@r3z. It's all part of the beautiful online experience.

Security Considerations

Although the differences between tethered and untethered are few, they are significant. For example, everyone has heard of the archetypal "black-hat packet sniffer," a giggling sociopath sitting on your physical Ethernet segment, surreptitiously logging packets for his own nefarious ends. This could be a disgruntled worker, a consultant with a bad attitude, or even (in one legendary case) a competitor with a laptop, time on his hands, and a lot of nerve.* Although switched networks, a reasonable working environment, and conscientious reception staff can go a long way to minimize exposure to the physical wiretapper, the stakes are raised with wireless. Suddenly, one

---

* As the story goes, a major computer hardware manufacturer once found a new "employee" sitting in a previously unoccupied cube. He had evidently been there for three weeks, plugged into the corporate network and happily logging data before HR got around to asking who he was.

---

no longer needs physical presence to log data: why bother trying to smuggle equipment onsite when you can crack from your own home or office two blocks away with a high-gain antenna?

Visions of cigarette smoking, pale-skinned über-crackers in darkened rooms aside, there is a point that many admins tend to overlook when designing networks: the whole reason that the network exists is to connect people to each other! Services that are difficult for people to use will simply go unused. You may very well have the most cryptographically sound method on the planet for authenticating a user to the system. You may even have the latest in biometric identification, full winnow and chaff capability, and independently verified and digitally signed content assurance for every individual packet. But if the average user can't simply check their email, it's all for naught. If the road to hell is paved with good intentions, the customs checkpoint must certainly be run by the Overzealous Security Consultant.

The two primary concerns when dealing with wireless clients are these:

- Who is allowed to access network services?
- What services can authorized users access?

As it turns out, with a little planning, these problems can be addressed (or neatly sidestepped) in most real-world cases. In this section, we'll look at some tools that can help keep your data flowing to where it belongs, as quickly and efficiently as possible.

WEP

The 802.11b specification outlines a form of encryption called wired equivalent privacy, or WEP. By encrypting packets at the MAC layer, only clients who know the "secret key" can associate with an AP or peer-to-peer group. Anyone without the key may be able to see network traffic, but every packet is encrypted.

The specification employs a 40-bit shared-key RC4 PRNG* algorithm from RSA Data Security. Most cards that use 802.11b (Proxim Orinoco, Cisco Aironet, Apple Airport, and Linksys WPC11, to name a few) support this encryption standard.

Although hardware encryption sounds like a good idea, the implementation in 802.11b is far from perfect. First of all, the encryption happens at the link layer, not at the application layer. This means your communications are protected up to the gateway, but no further. Once it hits the wire, your packets

---

* Pseudo-Random Number Generator. It could be worse, but entropy takes time.

are sent in the clear. Worse than that, every other legitimate wireless client who has the key can read your packets with impunity, since the key is shared across all clients. You can try it for yourself; simply run *tcpdump* on your laptop and watch your neighbor's packets just fly by, even with WEP enabled.

Many manufacturers have implemented their own proprietary extensions to WEP, including 104-bit keys and dynamic key management. Unfortunately, because they are not defined by the 802.11b standard, there is no guarantee that cards from different manufacturers that use these extensions will interoperate.

---

40 vs. 64 vs. 104 vs. 128-bit WEP

Why are so many different key lengths quoted by various card manufacturers? The original 802.11b spec defined a 40-bit user-specified key. This key is combined with a 24-bit initialization vector (the IV), a random number that is part of the WEP algorithm. Together, this yields 64 bits of "key," although the IV is actually sent in the clear!

Likewise, 104-bit WEP is used with the IV to yield 128 bits of "key." This is why user-defined keys are 5 characters long ($5 \times 8 = 40$) or 13 characters long ($13 \times 8 = 104$). The user doesn't define the IV; it is part of the WEP algorithm (and is generally implemented as 24 random bits).

More bits sounds more secure to the consumer, so some manufacturers choose to list the larger number as the "key length." Unfortunately, for WEP, having more bits does not guarantee significantly greater security. Read on.

To throw more kerosene on the burning WEP tire mound, a team of cryptographers at the University of California at Berkeley and other experts have identified weaknesses in the way WEP is implemented, and effectively these vulnerabilities have made the strength of encryption irrelevant. With all of its problems, why is WEP still supported by manufacturers? And what good is it for building public-access networks?

WEP was not designed to be the ultimate "killer" security tool (nor can anything seriously claim to be). Its acronym makes the intention clear: wired equivalent protection. In other words, the aim behind WEP was to provide no greater protection than you would have when you physically plug into your Ethernet network. (Keep in mind that in a wired Ethernet setting, there is no encryption provided by the protocol at all. That is what application layer security is for; see the tunneling discussion later in this chapter.)

What WEP does provide is an easy, generally effective, interoperable deterrent to unauthorized access. While it is technically feasible for a determined intruder to gain access, it is not only beyond the ability of most users, but usually not worth the time and effort, particularly if you are already giving away public network access!

As you'll see in Chapter 7, one area where WEP is particularly useful is at either end of a long point-to-point backbone link. In this application, unwanted clients could potentially degrade network performance for a large group of people, and WEP can not only help discourage would-be link thieves, but encourage them to set up more public-access gateways.

802.1x

802.1x is a fairly new IEEE specification. The full title of 802.1x is "802.1x: Port Based Network Access Control." Interestingly enough, 802.1x wasn't originally designed for use in wireless networks; it is a generic solution to the problem of port security. Imagine a college campus with thousands of CAT5 jacks scattered throughout libraries, classrooms, and computer labs. At any time, someone could bring their laptop on campus, sit down at an unoccupied jack, plug in, and instantly gain unlimited access to the campus network. If network abuse by the general public were common, it might be desirable to enforce a policy of port access control that permitted only students and faculty to use the network.

This is where 802.1x fits in. Before any network access (to Layer 2 or above) is permitted, the client (the *supplicant*, in 802.1x parlance) must authenticate itself. When first connected, the supplicant can exchange data only with a component called the *authenticator*. This in turn checks credentials with a central data source (the *authentication server*), typically a RADIUS server or other existing user database. If all goes well, the authenticator notifies the supplicant that access is granted (along with other optional data) and the client can go about its merry way. The various encryption methods employed are not defined, but an extensible framework for encryption (*EAP*, or *Extensible Authentication Protocol*) is provided.

802.1x has been widely regarded by the popular press as the fix for the problems of authentication in wireless networks. For example, the optional data that is sent back to the supplicant might contain WEP keys that are dynamically assigned per session. These keys could be automatically renewed every so often, making most data collection attacks against WEP futile. Unfortunately, 802.1x is susceptible to certain session hijacking methods, denial-of-service attempts, and man-in-the-middle attacks when used with wireless networks, making the use of 802.1x as the ultimate security tool a questionable proposition.

As of this writing, 802.1x drivers are available for Windows XP and 2000 and many access points (notably Cisco and Proxim) support some flavor of 802.1x. There is also an open source 802.1x implementation project available at *http://www.open1x.org/*.

How relevant is 802.1x to community wireless projects? It definitely depends on your goals. The vast majority of community projects incorporate open access points, with no authentication or encryption enabled. 802.1x could help provide a degree of security to a private wireless network (probably even better than WEP alone), although it shouldn't be considered a magic bullet. Combining 802.1x with a strong encrypted tunnel or VPN (see the upcoming section) will likely keep out the most tenacious of system crackers, but will make participation in your network much more difficult for casual users.

For a good discussion of 802.1x security methods and problems online, take a look at *http://www.sans.org/rr/wireless/80211.php*. Researchers at the University of Maryland have also published a paper on 802.11 security; it's available at *http://www.cs.umd.edu/~waa/wireless.html*.

Routing and Firewalls

The primary security consideration for wireless network access is where to fit it into your existing network. You need to consider what services you want your wireless users to be able to access, both on the Internet and on your internal network. Since the primary goal of this book is to describe methods for providing public access to network services (including access to the Internet), I strongly recommend setting up your wireless gateways in the same place you would any public resource: in your network's DMZ, or outside of your firewall altogether (as in Figure 3-5). This will give you the most flexibility in defining an internal security policy. Even in the absolute worst case of a complete breakdown of security precautions, the most that any social deviant will end up with is Internet access, and not unrestricted access to your private internal network.

This configuration leaves virtually no incentive for anyone to bother trying to compromise your gateway, as the only thing to be gained would be greater Internet access. Attacks coming from the wireless interface can easily log MAC address and signal strength information. With wireless, this can be a fair deterrent: because the would-be attacker needs to transmit to carry out an attack, they necessarily give away not only a unique identifier (their MAC address), but also their physical location!

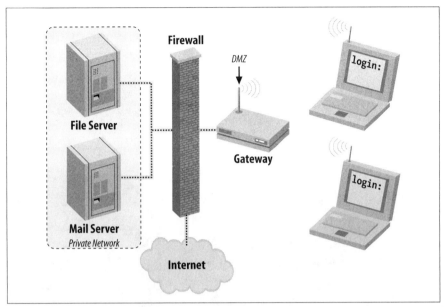

Figure 3-5. Place your wireless gateways outside of your private network!

Assuming that all wireless connectivity takes place outside of your private network, what happens when you or your friends want to connect from the wireless back into the inside? Won't other wireless users be able to just monitor your traffic and grab passwords and other sensitive information? Not if you use strong application-layer encryption.

Encrypted Tunnels

Application layer encryption is a critical technology when dealing with untrusted networks (such as public-access wireless links, for example). This is obvious when looking at a network diagram, as in Figure 3-6. When using an encrypted tunnel, you can secure your communications from eavesdroppers all the way to the other end of the tunnel.

If you're using a tunnel from your laptop to another server, would-be black hats listening to your conversation will have the insurmountable task of cracking strong cryptography. Until someone finds a cheap way to build a quantum computer (and perhaps a cold fusion cell to power it), this activity is generally considered a waste of time. In the previous example, a web server providing 128-bit SSL connections provides plenty of protection, all the way to your wireless laptop. SSL provides application layer encryption.

SSL is great for securing web traffic, but what about other network services? Take this typical scenario: you're at work or at home, merrily typing away

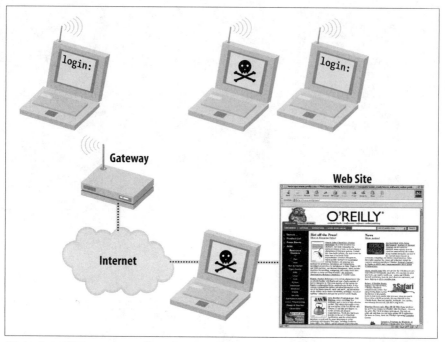

Figure 3-6. WEP encrypts only to the gateway, exposing your traffic to other wireless users and anything after the wire; tunnels protect your traffic from end to end

on your wireless laptop. You want to retrieve your email from a mail server with a POP client (Netscape Mail, Eudora, fetchmail, etc.). If you connect to the machine directly, your email client sends your login and password "in the clear." This means that a nefarious individual somewhere between you and your mail server (either elsewhere on your wireless network, or even "on the wire" if you are separated by another network) could be listening and could grab a copy of your information en route. This login could then be used not only to gain unauthorized access to your email, but in many cases will also grant a shell account on your mail server!

To prevent this, you can use the tunneling capabilities of SSH. An SSH tunnel works like this: rather than connecting to the mail server directly, we first establish an SSH connection to the internal network that the mail server lives in (in this case, the wireless gateway). Your SSH client software sets up a port-forwarding mechanism, so that traffic that goes to your laptop's POP port magically gets forwarded over the encrypted tunnel and ends up at the mail server's POP port. You then point your email client to your local POP port, and it thinks it is talking to the remote end (only this time, the entire session is encrypted). Figure 3-7 shows an SSH tunnel in a wireless network.

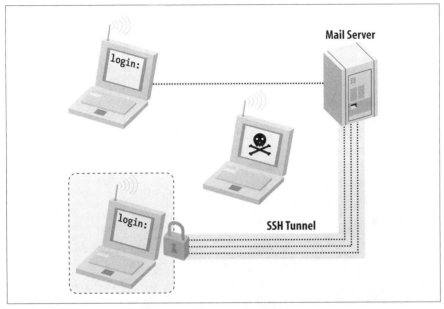

Figure 3-7. With an SSH tunnel in place, your otherwise-insecure conversation stays private

With the tunnel in place, anyone who tries to monitor the conversation between your laptop and the mail server will get something resembling line noise. It's a good idea to get in the habit of tunneling anything that you want to keep private, even over wired networks. SSH tunneling doesn't have to stop at POP connections either. Any TCP port (SMTP, for example) can easily be set up to tunnel to another machine running SSH, almost anywhere on the Internet. We'll see an example of how to do that in Chapter 7. For a full discussion of the ins and outs of this very flexible (and freely available) tool, I highly recommend *SSH, The Secure Shell: The Definitive Guide* (O'Reilly).

VPN

Using a virtual private network (VPN) is another popular method for dealing with wireless security shortcomings. Most VPN software uses powerful encryption and strong authentication to protect not only traffic to an individual port, but to all network traffic in general. If a wireless client is using good VPN software, all traffic from it can be well-protected, regardless of the security shortcomings of the underlying network. As with encrypted tunnels, sniffing the wireless traffic of a client associated with a public access point is possible, but will yield only strongly encrypted packets. While the tunnel server's IP address and amount of traffic being sent is still revealed, the actual data and ultimate destination of the user's traffic is still well-protected. Likewise, authentication credentials to otherwise unprotected services (such as unencrypted web and email passwords) are also protected.

Examples of popular VPN software include PPTP, *vtun*, IPSec tunnels, and even PPP over SSH. I highly recommend running strong VPN software as the only gateway back into your internal network, as this greatly simplifies access and sidesteps many security issues. Unfortunately, setting up VPN software is beyond the scope of this book, but there are many resources available online to assist you with this task. In general, VPN software is network agnostic, and will usually work with your wireless network without any additional configuration.

Other Potential Threats

If you are paranoid about security (as well you should be), there are a number of additional issues to consider when running open access points. The rules change considerably when people who have access to your physical infrastructure can't be trusted, particularly when Layer 2 network traffic can be easily and anonymously molested. I will discuss wireless security in more detail in Chapter 7, and offer some examples of common attacks, as well as describe the tools you can use to defend against them. For even more details, consult the excellent discussion of potential problems (and solutions) in *802.11 Security* (O'Reilly).

Summary

In order to maintain maximum compatibility with available 802.11b client hardware and yet still provide responsible access to the Internet, you can apply a combination of inexpensive hardware and freely available software to strike an acceptable balance between access and security.

In the following chapters, I'll show you how to set up basic wireless access to augment your existing wired network. I'll describe a workable method for providing wireless services to your local community, for minimal cost, while promoting community participation and individual responsibility.

## CHAPTER 4

Using Access Points

As we discussed in Chapter 3, an access point (AP) is a piece of hardware that connects your wireless clients to a wired network (and usually on to the Internet from there). As with any piece of bridging hardware, it has at least two network connections and shuffles traffic between them. The wireless interface is typically an on-board radio or an embedded PCMCIA wireless card. The second network interface can be Ethernet, a dialup modem, or even another wireless adapter. Many access points now even include multiple Ethernet ports, which simplifies the creation of a trusted network segment.

The access point hardware controls access to and from both networks. On the wireless side, most vendors have implemented 802.11b access control methods (such as WEP encryption keys, "closed" networks, and MAC address filtering). Some have added proprietary extensions to provide additional security, such as more sophisticated encryption.* Many access points also allow control over what the wired network can send to the wireless clients, through simple firewall rules. Much of this functionality is accessible through either a Java-based tool or a simple web page interface.

In addition to providing access control, the access point also maintains its own network connections. This includes functions such as dialing the phone and connecting to an ISP on demand, or using DHCP on the Ethernet interface to get a network lease. Most access points can provide NAT and DHCP service to the wireless clients, thereby supporting multiple wireless users while requiring only a single IP address from the wire. Some support direct bridging, allowing the wired and wireless networks to exchange data as if they were physically connected together. If the access point has multiple

---

* Unfortunately, as is usually the case with proprietary extensions, these services can be used only if all of your network clients are using hardware from the same vendor.

radios, it can bridge them together with the wire, allowing for a very flexible, extendable network.

Another important service provided by APs is the ability to "hand off" clients as they wander between access points. This lets users seamlessly walk around a college campus, for example, without ever dropping their network connection. Current AP technology allows roaming only between access points on the same physical subnet (that is, APs that aren't separated by a router). Unfortunately, the roaming protocol was left unimplemented in the 802.11 spec, so each manufacturer has implemented its own method. This means that hand-offs between access points of different manufacturers aren't currently possible.

In the last year, at least twenty different access point hardware solutions have hit the consumer market. Low-cost models (intended for home or small office use) such as the Linksys WAP11 and D-Link DWL-1000AP currently retail for around $75. Higher-end APs like the Proxim AP-2000 and Cisco Aironet 1200 cost about $600. Typically, higher-priced equipment includes more features, greater range, and generally more stable operations. While every AP will claim 802.11b (or Wi-Fi*) compliance, they are not all alike. Features that set different models apart include:

- Direct bridging to the wired network
- NAT/DHCP service
- Multiple radios (to support more users, or for use as a repeater)
- External antenna connectors
- Greater radio output power (most operate at 30mW, while some operate at 100mW or more)
- Security enhancements such as 802.1x and tagged VLANs
- Upgrade paths to 802.11g and 802.11a

In general, look for an AP in your price range that will work for your intended application, with the greatest possible range. Single radio APs can support several users simultaneously, and, as we'll see in Chapter 6, adding APs to your network is probably preferable to simply adding higher-gain antennas or amps to your existing AP.

---

* *Wi-Fi* is the "marketing friendly" name picked by the WECA (the Wireless Ethernet Compatibility Alliance) to refer to 802.11b-compliant gear. See *http://www.weca.net/* if you're so inclined.

Access Point Caveats

You should seriously consider how to balance ease of use with essential security when adding APs to your existing wired network. Even with WEP encryption and other access control methods in effect, AP security is far from perfect. Since an access point is by definition within range of all wireless users, every user associated with your access point can see the traffic of every other user. Unless otherwise protected (for example, with application layer encryption), all email, web traffic, and other data is easily readable by anyone running protocol analysis tools such as *tcpdump* or *ethereal*. As we saw in Chapter 3, relying on WEP alone to keep people out of your network may not be enough protection against a determined black hat.

In terms of establishing a community network, access points do provide one absolutely critical service: they are an easy, standard, and inexpensive tool for connecting wireless devices to a wired network. Once the wireless traffic hits the wire, it can be routed and manipulated just like any other network traffic, but it has to get there first.

Wireless access points that are on the consumer market today were designed to connect a small group of trusted people to a wired network and lock out everyone else. The access control methods implemented in the APs reflect this philosophy; if that is how you intend to use the gear, it should work very well for you. For example, suppose you want to share wireless network access with your neighbor, but not with the rest of the block. You could decide on a mutual private WEP key and private ESSID and keep them a secret between you. Since you presumably trust your neighbor, this arrangement could work for both of you. You could even make a list of all of the radios that you intend to use on the network and limit the access point to allow only them to associate. This would require more administrative overhead, as one of you would have to make changes to the AP each time you wanted to add another device, but it would further limit who could access your wireless network.

While a shared secret WEP key and static table of hardware MAC addresses may be practical for a home or small office, these access control methods don't make sense in a public-access setting. If you intend to offer network services to your local area, this "all or nothing" access control method is unusable. As we'll see in Chapter 7, it may be more practical to simply let everyone associate with your access point, and use other methods for identifying users and granting further access. These services take place beyond the AP itself (namely, at a router connected directly to the AP). See the "NoCat-Auth Captive Portal" discussion in Chapter 7. Such an arrangement requires a bit more equipment and effort to get started, but can support hundreds of people across any number of cooperative wireless nodes with very little administrative overhead.

Before we get too fancy, we have to understand how to configure an access point. Let's take a look at how to set up a very popular access point, the Apple AirPort.

The Apple AirPort Base Station

The AirPort is a tremendously popular access point (so popular, in fact, that there are a number of variations available: AirPort Graphite, AirPort Snow, and Airport Extreme). It looks like a slick, retro-futuristic prop from "War of the Worlds," and is very portable and rugged. While designed for use with the Mac platform, it works very well as a general-purpose access point (and you don't even need a Mac to configure it; see the next section). As I write this, the original Graphite AirPort sells retail for about $140. What does that get you?

- Direct Ethernet bridging
- DHCP / NAT
- 56k dialup modem port
- User-definable ESSID
- Roaming support
- MAC address filtering
- 40-bit WEP encryption

The Snow AirPort introduced an additional Ethernet port and more firewall options, as well as 104-bit WEP and completely redesigned internals. The new AirPort Extreme (about $199) comes equipped with all sorts of goodies, including two Ethernet ports, and most importantly, a draft 802.11g "Extreme" card. For $50 more, they throw in a USB port (for sharing a printer) and an external antenna connector.

All of the APs in the AirPort family have only one radio (an embedded Orinoco Silver card in the Graphite, an AirPort card in the Snow, and an "Extreme" mini-PCI card in the Extreme model). If you are thinking of adding a do-it-yourself antenna to a Graphite or Snow model, you definitely aren't the first. Take a look at the following URLs for details on how to retrofit an antenna onto the Graphite or Snow:

- *http://www.vonwentzel.net/ABS/ExtendedGraphite/index.html*
- *http://www.wwc.edu/~frohro/Airport/Airport.html*
- *http://www.vonwentzel.net/ABS/ExtendedSnow/index.html*

Out of the box, the AirPort will try to get a DHCP lease from a server somewhere on the Ethernet network, and start serving NAT and DHCP on the wireless, with no password. Yes, by simply plugging your new toy into your LAN, you have eliminated all of the hard work that went into setting up your firewall. Anyone within earshot now has unrestricted wireless access to the network you plugged it into!

While this could be handy at a conference or for any other public-access network, the default configurations are probably not what you want. To change them, you'll need configuration software. Thankfully, configuration of the various members of the AirPort family is remarkably similar. For the rest of this chapter, I'll assume that you are working with a classic Graphite AirPort.

Access Point Management Software

If you have a Mac handy, you are in luck. The AirPort Admin utility that ships with the AirPort is excellent. As with their entire product line, Apple has gone out of their way to make the whole AirPort system easy to set up, even for beginners. If you don't own a Mac, you have a couple of options. It turns out that the innards of the Graphite AirPort are virtually identical to the Orinoco RG-1000 (previously, the Lucent Residential Gateway). That means that the RG configuration utility for Linux (called *cliproxy*) also works fine with the AirPort. Unfortunately, as the Lucent product family has been sold and resold several times in the past couple of years (the same product line has been called Lucent, Orinoco, Agere, Avaya, and Proxim, and probably a couple of others that I've missed), the *cliproxy* utility seems to have disappeared from the Proxim web site. Copies of it are still floating around on various message boards; it is a tremendously useful utility if you can find it. Jon Sevy has done extensive work with the AirPort, and has released an open source Java client that configures the AirPort (both Graphite and Snow) and the RG-1000. You can get a copy from *http://edge.mcs. drexel.edu/GICL/people/sevy/airport/*. He has also compiled a tremendous amount if information on the inner workings of the AirPort, and has many resources online at this site. Since his utility is open source, cross-platform, and works very well, we'll use it in the following examples. Figure 4-1 shows the main screen of the Java Configurator.

To use the Java Configurator application, you'll need a copy of the Java Runtime Environment. Download it from *http://java.sun.com/*, if you don't already have it. You can start the utility by running the following in Linux:

```
$ java -jar AirportBaseStationConfig.jar &
```

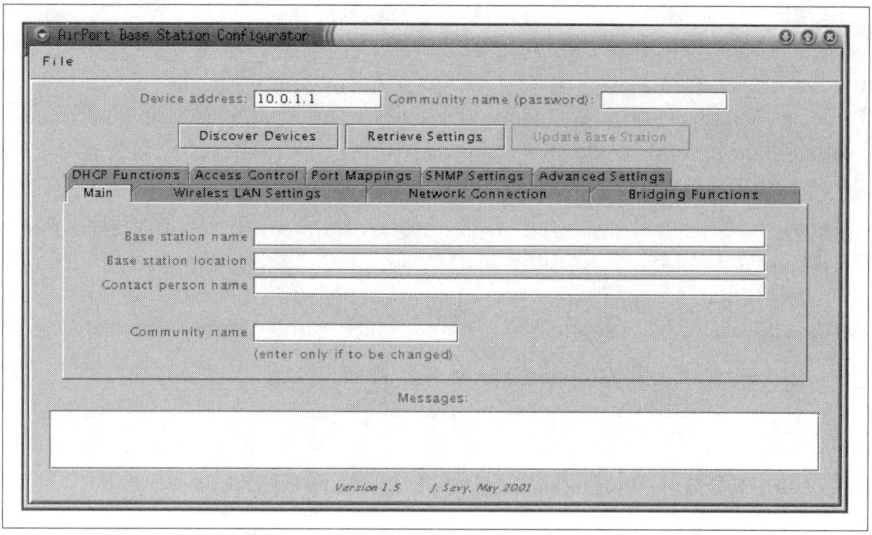

Figure 4-1. The AirPort Java Configurator

In Windows, start by double-clicking the AirportBaseStationConfig icon.

The AirPort can be configured over the Ethernet port or over the wireless network. When the application window opens, you can click the *Discover Devices* button to auto-locate all of the APs on your network. When you find the IP address of the AP you want to configure, type it into the *Device address* field, then type the password into the *Community name* field. If you're unsure about the IP address or the password, the AirPort ships with a default password of *public*, and an IP address of *10.0.1.1* on the wireless interface (it picks up the wired IP address via DHCP; use *Discover Devices* to find it if you're configuring it over the Ethernet). Once you've entered the correct information, click the *Retrieve Settings* button.

The very first thing you should change is the *Community name*, on the first panel. Otherwise, anyone can reconfigure your AirPort by using the *public* default! While you're there, you can set the name of the AirPort (which shows up in network scans), the location, and contact information. These fields are entirely optional, and have no effect on operations.

You should also choose a *Network name*, under the *Wireless LAN Settings* tab. This is also known as the ESSID, and will identify your network to clients in range. If you're running a "closed" network, it needs to be known ahead of time by any host attempting to connect, as described in the following section.

Local LAN Access

As stated earlier, the default AirPort configuration enables LAN access by default. If you're using DSL or a cable modem, or if you are installing the AirPort on an existing Ethernet network, this is what you want to use. In the Java Configurator, take a look at the *Network Connection* tab and check the *Connect to network through Ethernet port* radio button.

From here, you can configure the IP address of the AirPort, either via DHCP, by entering the IP information manually, or by using PPPoE. You'll probably want to use DHCP, unless your ISP requires a manual IP address or PPPoE.

Configuring Dialup

There is also a radio button on the *Network Connection* tab marked *Connect to network through modem*. Use this option if your only network connection is via dialup. Yes, it's very slow, but at least you're wireless. Note that the dialup and Ethernet choices are exclusive, and can't be used at the same time.

When you check *Connect to network through modem*, the pane prompts you for phone number, modem init string, and other dialup-related fields. Make sure that *Automatic dialing* is checked, so it will dial the phone when you start using the AirPort. Click on the *Username/Password/Login Script* button to enter your login information. On this screen, you can also define a custom login script, if you need to. The default script has worked fine for me with a couple of different ISPs.

Once the AirPort is configured for dialup, it will dial the phone and connect any time it senses Internet traffic on the wireless port. Just start using your wireless card as usual, and after an initial delay (while it's dialing the phone), you're online.

NAT and DHCP

By default, the AirPort acts as both a NAT server and a DHCP server for your wireless clients.* DHCP service is controlled by the *DHCP Functions* tab. To turn DHCP on, check the *Provide DHCP address delivery to wireless hosts* box. You can specify the range of IPs to issue; by default, the AirPort

---

* If you're just joining us, NAT and DHCP stand for *Network Address Translation* and *Dynamic Host Configuration Protocol*, respectively. See Chapter 3 for more details.

hands out leases between *10.0.1.2* and *10.0.1.50*. You can also set a lease time here. The lease time specifies the lifetime (in seconds) of an issued IP address. After this timer expires, the client reconnects to the DHCP server and requests another lease. The default of *0* (or unlimited) is probably fine for most installations, but you may want to set it shorter if you have a large number of clients trying to connect to your AirPort.

If you don't have another DHCP server on your network, the AirPort can provide service for your wired hosts as well. Check the *Distribute addresses on Ethernet port, too* box if you want this functionality.

 Check this box only if you don't have another DHCP server on your network! More than one DHCP server on the same subnet is a *bad* thing, and will bring the wrath of the sysadmin down upon you. Watching two DHCP servers duke out who gets to serve leases may be fun in your spare time, but can take down an entire network, and leave you wondering where your job went. What were you doing connecting unauthorized gear to the company network, anyway?

If you have more than one AirPort on the same wired network, make sure that you enable DHCP to the wire on only one of them and, again, only if you don't already have a DHCP server.

NAT is very handy if you don't have many IP addresses to spare (and these days, few people do). It also gives your wireless clients some protection from the wired network, as it acts as an effective one-way firewall (see Chapter 3 for the full story of NAT and DHCP). In the Configurator, NAT is set up in the *Bridging Functions* tab. To enable NAT, click the *Provide network address translation (NAT)* radio button. You can either specify your own private address and netmask, or leave the default (*10.0.1.1 / 255.255.255.0*).

Bridging

A big disadvantage to running NAT on your wireless hosts is that they become less accessible to your wired hosts. While the wireless users can make connections to any machine on the wire, connecting back through a NAT is difficult (the AirPort provides some basic support for this by allowing for static port mappings, but this is far from convenient). For example, if you are running a Windows client on the wireless, the Network Neighborhood will show other wireless clients only and not any machines on the wire, since NAT effectively hides broadcast traffic (which the Windows SMB protocol relies on). If you already have a DHCP server on your wired network, and are running private addresses, the NAT and DHCP functions of the AirPort are redundant, and can simply get in the way.

Rather than duplicate effort and make life difficult, you can disable NAT and DHCP and enable bridging to the wire. Turn off DHCP under *DHCP Functions* (as we saw previously), and check the *Act as transparent bridge (no NAT)* under the *Bridging Functions* tab. When the AirPort is operating in this mode, all traffic destined for your wireless clients that happens on the wire gets broadcast over wireless, and vice versa. This includes broadcast traffic (such as DHCP requests and SMB announcement traffic). Apart from wireless authentication, this makes your AirPort seem completely invisible to the rest of your network.

Once bridging is enabled, you may find it difficult to get the unit back into NAT mode. If it seems unresponsive to the Java Configurator (or Mac AirPort Admin utility) while in bridging mode, there are a couple of ways to bring it back.

If you have a Mac, you can do a manual reset. Push the tiny button on the bottom of the AirPort with a paper clip for about two seconds. The green center light on top will change to amber. Connect the Ethernet port on your AirPort to your Mac and run the *admin* utility. The software should let you restore the AirPort to the default settings. You have five minutes to do this before the amber light turns green and reverts to bridged mode.

If you're running Linux, you can easily bring the AirPort back online using Lucent's *cliproxy* utility, without needing a hard reset. Run the following commands from a Linux machine (either on the wire, or associated over the wireless):

```
$ cliproxy
[ORiNOCO]> show accesspoints
Searching...

Hostname      Eth Address     IP Address        Description
------------  --------------  ----------------  --------------------
NoCat         0030.42fa.cade  192.168.0.5       Base Station V3.64

[ORiNOCO]> configure remote 192.168.0.5 public
Config loaded from 192.168.0.5

NoCat> configure terminal

NoCat(config)> no service bridging

NoCat(config)> service napt

NoCat(config)> service dhcp-server
```

```
NoCat(config)> done

NoCat> write remote 192.168.0.5 public

NoCat> exit
```

Of course, substitute your password for *public* and IP address where applicable. At this point, the AirPort should reboot with NAT and DHCP enabled and bridging turned off.

If you're running Windows and need to reset an AirPort in bridged mode, I suggest you make friends with a Mac or Linux user. You might be able to get things back to normal by doing a hard reset (holding down the reset button with a paper clip for 30 seconds while powering the unit up), but I've never been able to make that work. The previous two methods—using a Mac hard reset or the Linux *cliproxy* utility—have worked well for me in the past. I keep a copy of *cliproxy* handy for just this reason.

WEP, MAC Filtering, and Closed Networks

If you really want to lock down your network at the access point, you have the following tools at your disposal: WEP encryption, filtering on MAC address (the radio card's serial number), and running a closed network. The three services are completely separate, so you don't necessarily have to run MAC filtering *and* a closed network, for example. Combining all of these features may not make your network completely safe from a determined miscreant, but will discourage the vast majority of would-be network hijackers.

To set the WEP keys, click the *Wireless LAN Settings* tab, and enter the keys in the fields provided. Also check *Use encryption* and uncheck *Allow unencrypted data* to require WEP on your network. Give a copy of this key to each of your wireless clients.

With MAC filtering enabled, the AirPort keeps an internal table of MAC addresses that are permitted to use the AirPort. Click the *Access Control* tab, and enter in as many MAC addresses as you like. Only radios using one of the MACs listed here will be allowed to associate with the AirPort. The MAC address of a radio card should be printed on the back of it (a MAC address consists of six hex numbers in the form 12:34:56:ab:cd:ef).

A closed network makes the AirPort refuse connections from radios that don't explicitly set the ESSID, i.e., clients with a blank ESSID, or one set to *ANY*. To make your network closed, check the *Closed network* box under *Wireless LAN Settings*.

Remember that without encryption, all traffic is sent in the clear, so anyone within range could potentially read and reuse sensitive information (such as ESSIDs and valid MAC addresses). Even with WEP, every other legitimate user can see this traffic. If you need to restrict access to a user later, you'll need to change the WEP key on every wireless client. But for small groups of trusted users, using these access control methods should discourage all but the most determined black hat without too much hassle.

Roaming

Wireless roaming can be very handy if your network is arranged in a way that you can support it. In order for roaming to be possible, your APs all need to be from the same manufacturer, they all need to reside on the same physical wired subnet (i.e., on the same IP network with no intervening routers), and all need to have the same *Network name* (ESSID).

In the AirPort, roaming is automatically enabled if all of these are true. Make sure that all of your AirPorts have the exact same *Network name* under *Wireless LAN Settings*. If for some reason you want to disable roaming, just give each AirPort a different ESSID.

Channel Spacing

In the 802.11b specification (in the United States), the 2.4GHz spectrum is broken into 11 overlapping channels. Ideally, as you add access points to your network, you want to allow your coverage areas (or *cells*) to overlap slightly, so there are no gaps in coverage. Wherever possible, you should keep a spacing of at least 25MHz (or 5 channels) in adjacent cells, as shown in Figure 4-2. Otherwise, traffic on nearby APs can interfere with each other, degrading performance.

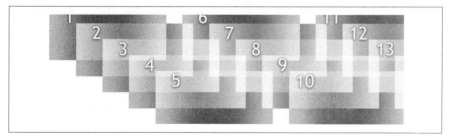

Figure 4-2. Channels are separated by at least 25MHz to prevent overlap and possible interference

For example, you may use channels 1, 6, and 11 in an alternating pattern to provide complete coverage without any frequency overlap. Of course, everyone else using 802.11b is trying to do the same thing, and they will probably be using one of these channels. Especially in a crowded area, perfect 25MHz spacing may be impossible. If necessary, you may be able to get away with spacing as close as two or three channels, but don't ever try to run two adjacent networks on the same channel (things may look fine at first, but will fall apart as the network load increases).

To figure out what channels your neighbors use, take a look at your signal strength meter and the other tools that your wireless card came with (the Orinoco/Agere/Proxim card, for example, ships with an excellent Site Map utility). You can also use NetStumbler, an excellent network discovery tool for Microsoft Windows. You can get it online for free at *http://www. netstumbler.com/*. I'll describe more tools that you can use for site surveys in Chapter 7.

## CHAPTER 5

Host-Based Networking

*If you want anything done well,
do it yourself. This is why most
people laugh at their own jokes.*
—Bob Edwards

An increasingly popular method for creating wireless networks is to forgo access point hardware entirely and use wireless cards directly in a host computer. The tremendous flexibility of free operating systems (such as Linux and BSD), combined with the ubiquity of inexpensive hardware, makes host-based networking the tool of choice for many large wireless projects. The added flexibility of such systems increases their complexity; if you're not already familiar with Linux, the details of this chapter might seem daunting. If you are just getting started with wireless networking, be sure to read the previous chapter on access points to see if they'll fit your needs.

Like a hardware access point, most useful host-based access points have at least two network interfaces: the wireless interface and one other interface. The second is typically an Ethernet device, although it can also be a modem, another radio, or any other network device. A computer can provide all of the typical access point functions, including DHCP, NAT, bridging, and MAC filtering. In addition, you have the entire suite of Linux applications and networking mechanisms at your disposal, allowing for all sorts of interesting features (including real routing, content-based packet filtering, dynamic intrusion detection, captive web portals, IPSEC tunnels, bandwidth throttling, and just about anything else you can think of).

The one critical technology that has been developed since the first edition of this book was released is the so-called Host AP driver, developed by Jouni Malinen. This software allows a Linux or BSD computer equipped with a wireless card to appear as if it were a true access point (that is, operate as a true *BSS Master*). While you can't use Host AP with every card on the market (in fact, it works only with cards that use the Prism chipset), it does perform surprisingly well. The Host AP driver allows the host computer to act as an AP for any 802.11b client, regardless of the manufacturer.

Another option for host-based networking is IBSS mode. As with Host AP, an IBSS network effectively makes expensive access point hardware entirely optional. Instead of a centralized model in which all clients must be within range of an access point in order to participate, IBSS allows any node to talk to another node within earshot. If one of those nodes happens to be a gateway to the Internet, it can also act as an access point and performs all typical access point functions.

The biggest disadvantage to IBSS is that, while nearly all client cards support IBSS mode, cards of different manufacturers don't always work together. This situation has improved in the last year, but cards are still not nearly as compatible in IBSS mode as they are when talking to a BSS Master. Also, some client software doesn't do such a good job of detecting available IBSS networks and, once associated, they rarely show signal and noise statistics.

Whenever possible, I highly recommend that you use the Host AP driver for host-based networking. You will reach the largest number of possible clients, and will be able to take advantage of all sorts of nifty features that are just creeping into the Host AP development tree. In this chapter, I'll show you how to build both a Host AP and an IBSS gateway using Linux.

Anatomy of a Wireless Gateway

To a Linux machine, the wireless card appears to be just another Ethernet device. The wireless driver in the kernel provides a network device (e.g., *eth0* or *wlan0*) that can do all of the things that any other network device can do. The rest of the system is completely unaware that communications are happening over radio. If you have ever built a firewall with Linux, much of this section should seem familiar to you.

If you haven't built a firewall with Linux, I highly recommend building one with old-fashioned Ethernet to get familiar with the process. O'Reilly's *Building Internet Firewalls, 2nd Edition* covers the specific networking issues involved in much greater detail than I have space for here. Another excellent document to work through is the Firewall and Proxy Server HOWTO at *http://www.linuxdoc.org/HOWTO/Firewall-HOWTO.html*.

Hardware

While Card Flash (CF), USB, PCI, and mini-PCI adapters have recently come to market, most 802.11b cards you will encounter are PCMCIA devices. At the time of this writing, wireless cards cost anywhere from $35–$100, with the average hovering around $65. Don't be fooled by their small size; these tiny cards are capable of sending a signal several miles with the proper antennas.

Obviously, to set up a machine as a wireless gateway using a PCMCIA card, you need a computer with at least one PCMCIA slot. Although the most common computers that support PCMCIA are laptops, a desktop or rack mount box with a PCMCIA converter card will also work. Many vendors sell PCMCIA to PCI or ISA converters specifically to fit wireless cards into desktop machines. There are also a number of inexpensive PCI cards on the market, including the Linksys WMP11 and the D-Link DWL-520. Both of these cards are supported by the Host AP driver.

If you have any doubts about whether your hardware is supported under Linux, consult the current Hardware HOWTO at *http://www.linuxdoc.org/ HOWTO/Hardware-HOWTO/*. There is also a lot of great information available in the Wireless HOWTO at *http://www.hpl.hp.com/personal/Jean_ Tourrilhes/Linux/Wireless.html*.

Note here that there are a bunch of older 802.11 frequency hopping cards floating around. They come in both PCMCIA and ISA/PCI packages and, unfortunately, are *not* 802.11b compliant. If you want to support 802.11b clients and data rates greater than 2Mbps, these cards will not help you. Always look for the "b" before you buy (there's a reason why the guy at the computer show is running a killer deal on $20 "wireless adapters").

In addition to a PCMCIA slot for the wireless adapter, you'll need an interface that connects to another network. In a laptop, this device is usually a network card in the second PCMCIA slot, although a built-in modem or Ethernet port will also work. In a desktop or rack mount machine, you can use any sort of network device but an Ethernet card is probably the most common (second only to dialup).

As far as actual computing hardware goes, you might consider using an older laptop or tablet PC as a gateway. It draws less power than a desktop, has built-in battery backup, and typically gives you two PCMCIA slots to work with. A 486 DX4/100 laptop can easily support several people as a masquerading gateway, as long as it has enough RAM (16 to 32MB should be plenty) and isn't doing anything other than routing packets and providing DHCP. We'll design our gateway to work "headless," so a working LCD panel won't be a requirement (assuming your laptop has an external video connector to initially configure it). You can often pick up older used laptops at thrift stores or computer surplus stores for under $200 (just be sure to try before you buy; it does need to boot!).

There are also a number of embedded-style computers that work quite well as host-based access points. Here are some examples of popular host hardware:

Soekris, *http://www.soekris.com/*
> A number of Soekris models work well as access points, with and without PCMCIA. All Soekris boards will boot from Compact Flash, and come standard with multiple Ethernet interfaces, a mini-PCI slot, hardware watchdog, serial console, and an AMD 133MHz processor. They are all fanless boards and use a DC power supply.

OpenBrick, *http://www.openbrick.org/*
> Another popular embedded solution is the OpenBrick. The typical OpenBrick has a 300MHz (fanless) Geode processor, boots from Compact Flash and has on-board NIC and PCMCIA slots. It runs on DC power and, unlike the Soekris, also has USB ports (although it does not have a mini-PCI slot).

Via-based computers, *http://www.via.com.tw/*
> There are a number of Via-based computers on the market. They are generally marketed as desktop PCs, although small fanless cases that take a DC power supply are becoming commonplace. Because they are intended for use as general-purpose PCs, they typically have 500MHz or better Via processors, on-board NICs, an IDE interface, USB, and a PCI slot. Using an inexpensive CF to IDE adapter, these boards (or indeed, any PC) can be modified to boot from Compact Flash. This offers a hardware solution with no moving parts.

The Fujitsu Stylistic series, *http://www.fujitsupc.com/*
> The Fujitsu Stylistic 1000 series is a very popular surplus market tablet PC that has "hack me" written all over it. It has three PCMCIA slots, one of which is the boot device. It can boot from Card Flash using a CF to PCMCIA adapter, and is unique in that it has an integrated LCD display and battery. The 1000 series has a 486 DX4/100 processor, is expandable to 40MB RAM, can use a cordless pen for input, and makes a fine hardware gateway (I use one myself for my node on SeattleWireless). Fujitsu still makes the Stylistic series, although new machines are quite expensive (on par with modern laptops). The older 1000s or 1200s can frequently be found on the surplus market for less than $100.

Whatever hardware platform you choose, be sure that it meets your needs. When choosing a piece of hardware, you should remember to consider the number and type of radio and network interfaces, cooling and power requirements, size, RAM and CPU available, and, of course, the cost. If you already have a machine on your network providing firewall services, it's a relatively simple matter to install a wireless adapter in it and have it serve as a gateway. If you already have a firewall running Linux, feel free to skip the following "Linux Distribution" section.

Linux Distribution

Choosing a distribution (much like choosing an operating system) should be a straightforward process: identify your project goals and requirements, assess what each of the competing choices provides, and make your choice. Unfortunately, the ultimate choice of "which one" seems to be increasingly driven by marketing machinery and passionate treatises on Usenet rather than simple design details.

Rather than settling on a particular Linux distribution (and accidentally revealing my tendency to Slack), here are some components that are absolutely vital to a wireless gateway, and should ideally be provided by your distribution.

Mandatory components:

- Linux 2.2 or 2.4 kernel
- The Host AP driver by Jouni Malinen, available online at *http://hostap. epitest.fi/*
- The Linux Wireless Tools Package by Jean Tourrilhes, available online at *http://www.hpl.hp.com/personal/Jean_Tourrilhes/Linux/Tools.html*
- PCMCIA-CS, if you are using PCMCIA radios
- Firewall tools (*ipchains* or *iptables*)
- A DHCP Server, such as the ISC's (*http://www.isc.org/products/DHCP/*) or *udhcpd* (*http://udhcp.busybox.net/*)
- Your favorite text editor

Optional components:

- SSH, for remote administration
- GCC (for compiling drivers and tools)
- PPP, for dialup ISP access
- DNS, Squid, and other typical caching network services

Some things you will not need (and they'd probably just get in the way):

- X Windows, including Gnome, KDE, or any other window manager
- Network services that you don't intend to provide on the gateway itself (NFS, Samba, print services, etc.)

Installing Linux is very straightforward with most modern distributions. Typically, simply booting from the CD will get the process going. I'll assume that you have the system installed and running on your existing network for the rest of this section. If you need help getting to your first login: prompt, there are tons of great references on how to install Linux online. You might start with the wealth of information from the Linux Documentation Project at *http://www.linuxdoc.org/*.

Of course, there are a number of existing Linux distributions that might allow you to skip the rest of this chapter altogether. For embedded solutions, there are a number of ready-to-run distributions specifically designed for wireless work. Two of the more popular distributions are Pebble (*http://www.nycwireless.net/pebble/*) and Leaf (*http://leaf.sourceforge.net/*). Pebble is a terrific project developed by Terry Schmidt of NYCWireless, and fits a very usable read-only, Debian-based Linux distribution (including Perl!) into less than 64MB of space. The WISP-Dist flavor of Leaf is designed to fit in under 16MB of space and includes many tools you need for a simple gateway.

In addition to embedded distributions, there are a few bootable CD distributions floating around that can easily be adapted for wireless work. The LinuxCare Bootable Toolkit (*http://lbt.linuxcare.com/*) and Knoppix (*http://www.knopper.net/knoppix/*) are two options. While a CD-ROM drive is obviously required, a hard drive or other storage medium is completely optional. All too frequently, community projects are centered around "what can we do with what we have" rather than "what can we buy to do what we want." If you have a pile of donated equipment and much of it can boot from CD, one of these distributions might be exactly what you need.

Kernel Configuration

Once your system software is installed, you'll need to configure the kernel to provide wireless drivers and firewall services. The parameters that need to be set depend on which kernel you're running. The 2.2 kernel has been around for quite a while and has proven itself stable in countless production environments. The 2.4 kernel is up to 2.4.20 as of this writing. While much more rich in features and functionality, it is also a much larger and more complex piece of software. For a new installation on a machine with adequate RAM (at least 16MB for a simple gateway), the 2.4 kernel is probably the best choice, as more and more developers are actively developing drivers for this platform. If space is tight, or you have an existing machine running 2.2 that you would like to turn into a gateway, 2.2 works fine in most cases.

Let's look at the specific kernel parameters that need to be set for each kernel. In either case, first *cd* to your Linux source tree and run *make menuconfig*. For these examples, we'll assume you're using either 2.2.23 or 2.4.20. Feel free to compile any of these options as loadable modules.

Linux 2.2.23

In addition to drivers specific to your hardware (SCSI or IDE drivers, standard filesystems, etc.), make sure the following parameters are compiled into the kernel:

Under *Loadable module support:*

- Enable loadable module support

Under *Networking options:*

- Packet socket
- Network firewalls
- Socket filtering
- IP: firewalling
- IP: masquerading
- IP: ICMP masquerading (if you want to use tools such as *ping* and *traceroute*)

Under *Network device support:*

- Wireless LAN (non-ham radio)

Note that you need to enable only the Wireless LAN category, not any of the specific drivers. This enables the kernel's Wireless Extensions, and provides the */proc/net/wireless* monitoring interface. Don't worry about PCMCIA network drivers as these will be provided by the PCMCIA-CS package or the Host AP driver.

Linux 2.4.20

Verify that the following are built into your kernel:

Under *Loadable module support:*

- Enable loadable module support

Under *General setup:*

- Support for hot-pluggable devices

This enables the *PCMCIA/CardBus support* category. Under that section, enable the following:

- PCMCIA/CardBus support
- CardBus support (only if you have a CardBus network card, i.e., most 100baseT cards)
- Support for your PCMCIA bridge chipset (most are i82365, although it generally doesn't hurt to compile in both)

Under *Networking options:*

- Packet socket
- Network packet filtering
- Socket filtering
- TCP/IP networking

This enables the *IP: Netfilter Configuration* category. Under that section, enable the following:

- Connection tracking
- FTP protocol support
- IP tables support
- Packet filtering
- Full NAT
- MASQUERADE target support

Under *Network device support* there are two subcategories of interest. Under *Wireless LAN (non-hamradio)* enable:

- Wireless LAN (non-hamradio)

Also enable support for any PCMCIA radio cards you intend to use here. If you want to use Host AP for your Prism-based radio, don't worry. We'll build that after we're finished with the kernel. I prefer to build these as modules, but you can build them into the kernel as well.

Under *PCMCIA network device support*, be sure to enable the following:

- PCMCIA network device support
- PCMCIA Wireless LAN
- Any PCMCIA network drivers for your hardware

Beyond these required components, include the drivers you need for your specific hardware. If this is your first time building a new kernel, remember to keep things simple at first. The dazzling assortment of kernel options can be confusing, and trying to do too many things at once may lead to conflicts that are difficult to pin down. Just include the minimum functionality you need to get the machine booted and on the network, and worry about adding fancy functionality later. The Linux Documentation Project has some terrific reference and cookbook-style material in the Kernel HOWTO at *http://www.linuxdoc.org/HOWTO/Kernel-HOWTO.html*. RTFM[*] and encourage others to do the same!

PCMCIA-CS

PCMCIA and Card Services provide operating system support for all kinds of credit card–sized devices, including Ethernet and wireless cards. The PCMCIA-CS package is actually made up of two parts: the drivers themselves and utilities that manage loading and unloading the drivers. The utilities detect when cards are inserted and removed and can give you status information about what has been detected.

If you are using a non-PCMCIA radio card, you can configure the card just as you would any other network device. As methods vary wildly between distributions, consult your distribution documentation for configuration options.

Software

If your distribution includes a recent release of PCMCIA-CS, feel free to skip this section. You can tell what version you have installed by running */sbin/cardmgr -V*. The latest (and recommended) release as of this writing is 3.2.3.

If you need to upgrade your PCMCIA-CS, follow the installation instructions in the package (it comes with a current version of the PCMCIA-HOWTO). When building from source, the package expects you to have your kernel source tree handy, so build your kernel first and then PCMCIA-CS. You can download the latest release at *http://pcmcia-cs.sourceforge.net*.

Configuration

Setting up radio parameters is very straightforward. All of the wireless parameters are set in */etc/pcmcia/wireless.opts*.

---

[*] Read The Fine Manual. Thanks to the efforts of volunteer groups such as the LDP and thousands of contributors, Linux has become possibly the best documented operating system on the planet. And where the Fine Manual isn't available, the Source is. Read it.

Here's an example *wireless.opts* for IBSS mode:

```
#
# wireless.opts
#

case "$ADDRESS" in

*,*,*,*)
    INFO="Any card in IBSS mode"
    ESSID="NoCat"
    MODE="Ad-Hoc"
    RATE="auto"
    ;;

esac
```

Here's another example for BSS Master (i.e., Host AP) mode:

```
#
# wireless.opts
#

case "$ADDRESS" in

*,*,*,*)
    INFO="A card in Host AP Master mode"
    ESSID="NoCat"
    MODE="Master"
    CHANNEL="6"
    RATE="auto"
    ;;

esac
```

You may be thinking, "My God, it's full of stars..." But if you have ever worked with *network.opts*, the syntax is exactly the same. If you haven't, those asterisks allow for tremendous flexibility.

The script is passed a string in *$ADDRESS* that gives details about the card that was inserted, so you can have different entries for different cards. The address-matching syntax is:

```
scheme, socket, instance, MAC address)
```

The *scheme* allows for setting up as many arbitrary profiles as you like. The most common use for schemes is on a client laptop, where you may have different network settings for your office wireless network than for your home network. You can display the current scheme by issuing the *cardctl scheme* command as root, and you can change it by using a command like *cardctl scheme home* or *cardctl scheme office*. Both *wireless.opts* and *network. opts* are scheme-aware, allowing you to change your network and wireless settings quickly with a single command.

The second parameter, *socket*, is the socket number that the PCMCIA card was inserted into. Usually, they start with 0 and go up to the number of PCMCIA slots you have available. To find out which is which, insert a card in one slot and issue the *cardctl status* command.

The third parameter, `instance`, is used for exotic network cards that have more than one interface. I haven't come across one of these, but if you have a network card that has more than one network device in it, use this to set different parameters for each device, starting with 0.

I find the last parameter, `MAC address`, very useful, as you can match the setting to a specific MAC address. You can even include wildcards to match a partial MAC address, like this:

```
*,*,*,00:02:2D:*)
```

This would match any recent Lucent card inserted in any slot, in any scheme. Keep in mind that the *wireless.opts* is called only to set radio parameters. Network settings (such as IP address, default gateway, and whether to use DHCP) are set in *network.opts*.

For our wireless gateway example, we'll need to set up an Ethernet card and a wireless card. Include the previous code in your *wireless.opts*. Create entries in your *network.opts* like these:

```
*,0,*,*)
    INFO="Wired network"
    DHCP="y"
    ;;

*,1,*,*)
    INFO="Wireless"
    IPADDR="10.0.0.1"
    NETMASK="255.255.255.0"
    NETWORK="10.0.0.0"
    BROADCAST="10.0.0.255"
    ;;
```

Be sure to put these above any section that starts with *,*,*,*) as it will preempt your specific settings. These settings assume that the wired network will get its IP address via DHCP. You can set DHCP="n" (or just remove the line) and include IP address information as in the second example if your ISP uses static IPs. The examples assume that the Ethernet card is in slot 0, and the radio is in slot 1. You could also match the MAC address of your cards if you want the flexibility to plug either card in either slot, although generally, once your gateway is up and running you'll want to forget it's even on. See the PCMCIA-HOWTO for full details on all of the tricky things you can do with *$ADDRESS*.

Host AP

The Host AP driver allows a Prism-based radio card to operate as a BSS master or slave, and it can also use IBSS mode. It is highly recommended that you use a 2.4 Linux kernel if you use Host AP. To get started with Host AP, download the driver at *http://hostap.epitest.fi/*.

Once the driver is unpacked, simply run a *make* with the name of the driver you want to build: *make pccard* builds the PCMCIA driver, *make plx* builds the non-PCMCIA (plx-based) PCI PC Card driver, and *make pci* builds the PCI driver. The hardware-independent driver code is automatically built regardless of the driver you choose. It doesn't hurt to build all of the drivers, unless space is a critical consideration on your system. To install the drivers, run *make install_pccard*, *make install_plx*, or *make install_pci* respectively.

If you are installing the PCMCIA driver, the *make* process automatically copies *hostap_cs.conf* to your */etc/pcmcia/* directory, so that your cards are properly detected when they are inserted. It doesn't hurt to stop and start PCMCIA services once you have installed the Host AP driver. Once installed, the wireless device will be called *wlan0* (and the second is called *wlan1*, etc.).

Wireless Tools

The excellent Wireless Tools package is maintained by Jean Tourrilhes. You can get it online at *http://www.hpl.hp.com/personal/Jean_Tourrilhes/Linux/Tools.html*.

From his page:

> The Wireless Extension is a generic API allowing a driver to expose to the user space configuration and statistics specific to common Wireless LANs.

These tools provide a method of controlling the parameters of a wireless card, regardless of what kind of card is installed (assuming that the wireless card driver uses the kernel's wireless extensions). It allows you to set the ESSID, WEP keys, operating mode (BSS or IBSS), channel, power saving modes, and a slew of other options. Simply unpacking the archive and running *make; make install* should copy the binaries to */usr/local/sbin* (see the installation notes in the package for more details). The tools currently bundled in Version 21 are *iwconfig, iwspy, iwlist,* and *iwpriv.* They are absolutely necessary for any Linux gateway or client.

Like its networking counterpart *ifconfig,* the *iwconfig* tool operates on a specific interface and lets you view or change its parameters. You can run it at any time from the command line as root to see what's going on. In addition,

PCMCIA-CS calls *iwconfig* when a card is inserted in order to set the initial parameters.

Here's a typical *iwconfig* output:

```
root@entropy:~# iwconfig eth0

eth0      IEEE 802.11-DS  ESSID:"NoCat"  Nickname:"Entropy"
          Mode:Ad-Hoc  Frequency:2.412GHz  Cell: 00:02:2D:FF:00:22
          Bit Rate:11Mb/s   Tx-Power=15 dBm   Sensitivity:1/3
          RTS thr:off   Fragment thr:off
          Encryption key:off
          Power Management:off
          Link Quality:56/92  Signal level:-40 dBm  Noise level:-96 dBm
          Rx invalid nwid:0  invalid crypt:0  invalid misc:0
```

As you can see, *eth0* is a wireless device. The ESSID is set to "NoCat" and WEP encryption is off. For security reasons, the encryption parameter is shown only if *iwconfig* is run by root. If there are any other wireless cards in range with the same parameters set, they can see this node and communications can commence, exactly as if they were on the same physical piece of wire. Run a *man iwconfig* for the full list of parameters. The *iwconfig* binary should be in a common binary path (such as */usr/sbin* or */usr/local/sbin*) for PCMCIA-CS to be able to use it.

The other tools allow nifty features such as monitoring the relative signal strength of other IBSS nodes, showing available frequencies and encoding bit rates, and even setting internal driver parameters, all from the command line. See the documentation for the full details, and some more examples in Chapter 7.

For most operations involving a wireless gateway, the *iwconfig* tool will provide all of the functionality we need to program the wireless card. While you're at Jean Tourrilhes' site, pick up a copy of *hermes.conf* and copy it to */etc/pcmcia*. It will tell PCMCIA to use the new *orinoco_cs* driver (rather than the older *wvlan_cs*) for all compatible radios. See his site documentation for more details.

Masquerading

From the *IP-Masquerade-HOWTO* document (available at *http://www. linuxdoc.org/HOWTO/IP-Masquerade-HOWTO.html*):

> IP Masq is a form of Network Address Translation or NAT that allows internally connected computers that do not have one or more registered Internet IP addresses to have the ability to communicate to the Internet via your Linux box's single Internet IP address.

IP masquerading makes it almost trivial to give an entire private network access to the Internet, while only using one official, registered IP address.

By configuring the gateway's wired Ethernet to use your ISP-assigned address and enabling masquerading between the wireless and the wire, all of your wireless clients can share the Internet connection as shown in Figure 5-1. The internal hosts think they're connected directly to the Internet, and there is no need to specially configure any applications (as you would with a traditional proxy server).

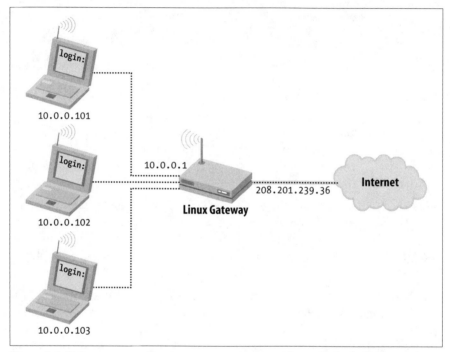

Figure 5-1. Using masquerading, an entire private network can "hide" behind a single real IP address

As with any form of NAT, masquerading isn't without its drawbacks. For example, the connectivity is one-way by default. Internal hosts can connect to Internet resources, but users from the Internet cannot connect to internal nodes directly.

To configure masquerading for the 2.2.23 kernel, save the following script to /etc/rc.d/rc.firewall (or /etc/init.d/firewall, depending on your distribution), and add a call to it in one of your startup scripts:

```
#!/bin/sh

echo "Enabling IP masquerading..."

# Set the default forwarding policy to DENY
/sbin/ipchains -P forward DENY

# Enable masquerading from the local network
/sbin/ipchains -A forward -s 10.0.0.0/24 -j MASQ

# Turn on forwarding in the kernel (required for MASQ)
echo "1" > /proc/sys/net/ipv4/ip_forward
```

For Linux 2.4.20, install these commands in the same place, but use *iptables* to set up the masquerading rules:

```
#!/bin/sh

echo "Enabling IP Masquerading..."
/sbin/iptables -t nat -A POSTROUTING -o eth0 -j MASQUERADE

# Turn on forwarding in the kernel (required for MASQ)
echo "1" > /proc/sys/net/ipv4/ip_forward
```

Be sure to substitute *eth0* with the interface name of your wireless card. Of course, this is a very simple example; feel free to elaborate on these rules according to your particular needs and desires. You can also get a copy of these sample scripts at: *http://examples.oreilly.com/wirelesscommnet2/*.

These rules enable anyone within range of your radio to masquerade behind your live IP address and access the Internet as if they were directly connected.

DHCP Services

As we saw in Chapter 3, DHCP lets network clients automatically discover the proper network parameters without human intervention. If we want our wireless clients to use DHCP, we need to provide it on the wireless interface.

The standard DHCP server was written by the Internet Software Consortium. If it wasn't provided by your distribution, pick up a copy at *http:// www.isc.org/products/DHCP/*. Configuration is very straightforward. Just create an */etc/dhcpd.conf* with the following information:

```
subnet 10.0.0.0 netmask 255.255.255.0 {
    range 10.0.0.100 10.0.0.200;
    option routers 10.0.0.1;
    option domain-name-servers 1.2.3.4;
}
```

Substitute 1.2.3.4 with your local DNS server.

Once that is in place, add an entry in your */etc/rc.d/rc.local* script to call *dhcpd* on the wireless interface. Assuming your wireless card is at *eth0*, this should do it:

```
echo "Starting dhcpd..."
/usr/sbin/dhcpd eth0
```

If *dhcpd* complains about a missing *dhcp.leases* file, try *touch /var/state/dhcp/dhcpd.leases* as root, and start it again. See the documentation for more troubleshooting techniques and examples, including how to set up static leases, WINS servers, groups, and all sorts of things you probably never thought a DHCP server could be capable of.

Make sure you run *dhcpd* on your wireless interface, and not on the wire! Since *dhcp* is a broadcast protocol, a network can have at most one *dhcp* server. More than one can cause all sorts of network nastiness as the two duke it out each time a client requests a *dhcp* lease.

There a few free alternatives available to the standard ISC *dhcpd*. One interesting package is *udhcpd*, available at *http://udhcp.busybox.net/*. While it doesn't have nearly the bells, whistles, and vibraslaps (*http://www.helixmusic.com.au/vibraslap.htm*) of the ISC's implementation, it does provide simple DHCP service very, very quickly.

If you would rather use your existing network's DHCP server, you might consider Layer 2 bridging. There are great examples of how to accomplish bridging in the Host AP package (in the *README.prism2* file) and at *http://bridge.sourceforge.net/*. Generally speaking, a routed access point is more efficient than a bridged access point because it can help prevent unnecessary traffic from being broadcast over the air. But if you are the adventurous type, jump in and give it a try. If your wireless card supports Layer 2 bridging, you can configure it for bridging just like any other network interface.

Security

The examples shown earlier create a simple, open gateway configuration. If you don't care who associates with your gateway (and uses your network), this configuration should work fine for you. An example of such a public-access service would be at a conference or user group meeting, or in a community network project. In these cases, many clients will be connecting to the network and ease of connection is the primary concern.

In other circumstances, you may not want to allow just any stranger to use your network. Suppose you wanted a wireless gateway for your network at home, and you set up the gateway to use your DSL line's external IP address. Anyone who was within range of your radio could potentially connect, drain your bandwidth, and even send spam or attack other machines on the network. All of this traffic would originate from your IP address, which you are contractually (not to mention socially) responsible for.

If you want to simply allow access for yourself and your friends, enabling WEP encryption can serve as an easy and effective deterrent to would-be network hijackers. When using a WEP, all clients that want to talk to each other must use the same key. In most clients, it can be specified either as a hexadecimal number, or as an ASCII string. The length of the key depends on the level of encryption you want to use. As the 802.11b spec allows for 40-bit keys, using it will allow any kind of hardware that complies with the specification to communicate with each other. Some manufacturers have released their own 128-bit encryption implementations, but because it isn't part of the current standard, such cards will work only with equipment of the same manufacturer.

I highly recommend using 40-bit encryption for simple access control, as it will cause fewer compatibility issues later. As we've seen, simply adding more bits to a key doesn't necessarily do much for greater security.

To use 40-bit keys in Linux, specify either a 5-character string or a 10-digit hexadecimal number as the *enc* parameter to *iwconfig*. Many people like to use strings because they're easier to remember. If you do use an ASCII string, you need to preface it with *s:* to tell *iwconfig* that a string follows. If you want to set the key to the ASCII string pLan9, you could use either of these two commands:

```
root@gateway# iwconfig eth0 enc s:pLan9
root@gateway# iwconfig eth0 enc 704C-616E-39
```

Note that when using ASCII keys, the key is case-sensitive.

To enable WEP on your gateway at boot time, edit your */etc/pcmcia/wireless. opts* to add a *KEY=* line to your wireless section, like this:

```
KEY="s:pLan9"
```

Remember that when making changes to files in */etc/pcmcia/*, it is necessary to stop and start PCMIA services (or reboot) before the changes become active. See the earlier "PCMCIA-CS" section for full details on how to set up *wireless.opts*.

Once your gateway is set up, give your private key to all of the wireless clients that you want to grant access to. As long as the ESSID and WEP keys match, you can have a private network that provides Internet access. Other radios in the area cannot use your gateway without this information.

If your intent is to offer network access to your local area without exposing yourself to risk or giving away all of your bandwidth, take a look at the "NoCatAuth Captive Portal" section of Chapter 7.

Putting It All Together

To recap everything that goes into building the gateway:

- Install the hardware.
- Configure the kernel.
- Upgrade PCMCIA-CS, if needed.
- Install Host AP, if needed.
- Install Wireless Tools.
- Check */etc/pcmcia/wireless.opts* and *network.opts*, setting the ESSID, network parameters, and WEP keys (if needed).
- Set up firewalling rules for masquerading.
- Set up *dhcpd* to start at boot.

Once all of that is in place, reboot the gateway to be sure everything initializes properly without human intervention. Congratulations, you now have a wireless gateway! Now that you can talk to wireless clients with your host-based AP, your imagination is the limit. Some innovative networking techniques are provided in Chapter 7.

## CHAPTER 6

Long-Range Networking

You have an access point. Your laptop is humming merrily along. While working at home or the office is more flexible than ever, you find yourself wondering what it would take to get a signal across the street, at your favorite coffee shop.

Or maybe you live in an area where you're on the perpetual "we'll get back to you" list for broadband services such as DSL and cable modems and you're ready to make it happen now. With the right equipment, enough participants, and the cooperation of the lay of the land, you can make broadband Internet access a reality in your neck of the woods.

Whatever your motivations, you are looking for a way to extend 802.11b beyond the listed 300-meter limit. This is not only possible and completely legal, it's also a lot of fun. You first need to figure out what your target coverage area is, and what resources you need to make it happen.

While extending your private network for an extra block or two (or even several miles, with the proper antennas) may be interesting for you, it does nothing for those around you except generate more noise in the band. Most people will find it prohibitively expensive to rent tower space and set up network access for themselves, for wherever they happen to be in town. This has led to the fascinating phenomenon of the cooperative wireless network.

The single best piece of advice I can give you on your journey to the ultimate network (whether public or private) is to fight the urge to blindly go it alone. Get people from your local neighborhood involved. Call a general meeting of interested parties. Find other people in your area who are interested in similar goals, and get your resources together. If there aren't any, join the development lists of any of the major community network groups (see Chapter 8) and ask around. Chances are, others have done (or are contemplating doing) what you want to do, and they'll probably be more than happy to share their experiences.

As the number of people interested in wireless network access increases, a public-access network stands to benefit by access to more vantage points, both figurative and physical. While you might not have direct line of sight to a place you want to talk to, your neighbor might. And for complementary network access, they might just be willing to let you install some equipment and use their house as a repeater. Wireless bandwidth costs only electricity and equipment, not telephone or cable company charges. This kind of massively parallel, cooperative arrangement is what makes a high-speed wireless wide area network possible. However, I can only give you the technical details: the social details are left as an exercise to the reader.

Topo Maps 102: Geographical Diversity

If you want to stretch your signal more than just across the street, you're going to have to consider exactly what lies between each point of your network. In Chapter 2, we looked at using USGS topographic maps and DOQs to estimate how the land lies between two arbitrary points. In addition to paper and online topographic maps, CD-ROM versions have been around for a few years. While typically geared toward hikers and outdoors enthusiasts, they have a lot to offer the aspiring wide area network engineer.

Software

I have evaluated two popular commercial topo packages, Topo! by National Geographic, and DeLorme's TopoUSA 2.0. While they're both packed with features, only a few are directly applicable to helping analyze land between two points. Figure 6-1 shows a Topo! rendering of Sebastopol, California.

Here are some points to keep in mind when evaluating topo software for link analysis:

- The software should provide cross-section views of a route or drawn trail. This is probably the feature used most often in trying to figure out if the land will cooperate (see the next section for examples).

- Almost any self-respecting topo software package includes the ability to mark up the maps with points and text. The ability to import latitudinal and longitudinal data and translate it into data points is handy if you know a site only by that information.

- If you intend to use a GPS with your software (see the next section), make sure your topo software supports your GPS hardware. Both packages I evaluated support most popular GPS hardware and the NMEA data standard (which virtually all modern GPS receivers speak).

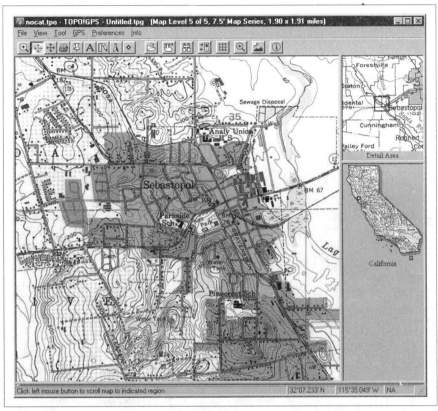

Figure 6-1. A Topo! rendering of Sebastopol, CA

- Both packages that I currently use are for Windows only. There are lots of Linux mapping packages floating about that render USGS DOQs and DEMs, but, like a lot of Linux software, it may take a bit of fiddling to get them going. Check out the mapping resource links at the major community wireless sites listed in Chapter 8, as this is an area of rapid development in the open source community.

Whatever software you choose, it should make it easy to weed out, at a glance, the obviously impossible direct links. If you get a "maybe" (which is frequently the case), you'll just have to go out and try it. Of course, for most of us, that's the fun part.

Using a GPS to Log Prospective LAT / LONG / ALT

Whenever I visit a potential node site, I bring my GPS with me. It logs not only the (more or less) precise latitude and longitude, but also the altitude of the site. This is data you can estimate with a topo map, but it can be handy to have in a precise measurement (particularly if you have logged several points in your intended network path). Figure 6-2 shows the use of GPS to tag potential sites.

Figure 6-2. You can use a GPS to tag potential sites and analyze them later in software

After collecting points, you can pull them into your topo software and plot them. Draw routes between them to figure out how the land lies between the two points. Figure 6-3 shows a Topo! rendering of a site. Based on this representation, the shot should be a piece of cake.

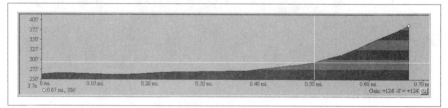

Figure 6-3. Good topo software should be able to give you a cross-section lay of the land between any two points

Keep in mind that, although the topo software has surveyed geological data, it won't have tree or building information. You can get a general idea of how cluttered an area is, but you won't really know until you try the shot. Using the overhead view in conjunction with the cross section, you can not only weed out the obvious negatives, but also find potential workarounds. Figure 6-4 shows a site that wouldn't work. Maybe you can go around it? Who lives on that hill, anyway?

Using the overhead view to locate key repeater points can be fun. Find out where the good sites are, and try contacting the people at those points. More often than not, people are willing to work with local community groups to provide free access (particularly if they don't have to do much besides provide electricity while getting free high-speed access).

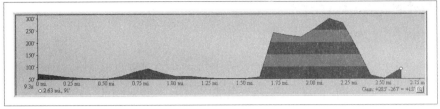

Figure 6-4. This cross section shows the long-distance nightmare: no chance

Plotting the Points on a 3-D Map

DeLorme has the interesting ability to create 3-D renderings of a topo region, complete with data markers and labels (Figure 6-5). While it's a really cool feature (and is very catchy in presentations), it has limited practical value beyond helping to visualize the surrounding terrain.

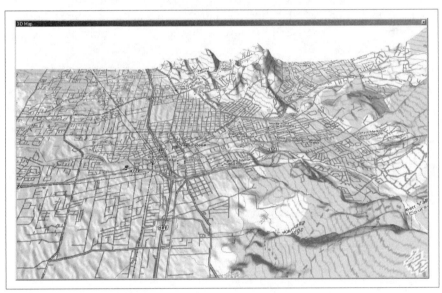

Figure 6-5. DeLorme's TopoUSA gives you a 3-D rendering of any topo region, complete with data points

Generally speaking, the more data points you collect, the more impressive your visual presentation will be.

Once your points are plotted on a map, you can very quickly determine which sites are worth developing. If you can't get direct line of sight to a place you'd like, take a look at the surrounding geography and see if you can find another way. If you can't go through, you'll have to go over or around. Software topo maps can make finding the "bank shots" much easier.

Antenna Characteristics and Placement

While I am not a radio frequency (RF) engineer, I have had a lot of practical experience setting up 802.11b networks. There isn't nearly enough room here for a full examination of the nuances of radio frequency communications. For more authoritative sources, be sure to check out the great resources in the Appendixes. Radio is an entire field of study unto itself.

Antenna selection has a tremendous impact on the range and usability of your wireless network. Ironically, the design of almost every external 802.11b card puts the antenna in the worst possible orientation: sideways and very close to the laptop (or desktop). In this position, the radiation pattern is almost straight up and down! Not only does this drive half of your signal into the table, it leaves your poor, underpowered radio susceptible to interference from the computer itself. Fortunately, laptop manufacturers have responded to this problem, and are now following Apple's lead in building antennas into their screens and cases.

You will see a tremendous difference in signal strength by attaching a small omnidirectional external antenna to your client card and orienting it properly. Which way is proper? That depends on your environment. If you are having trouble pulling in a signal, try every possible position with your signal strength meter open. I've put mine on top of my monitor, below the desk, sideways, on the table behind me, and even slung over my shoulder. The best orientation of your antenna is the position in which it receives the best signal—don't be afraid to move it around.

If you use a PCMCIA radio and are without an external antenna, you can watch the wonders of RF by opening up your strength meter and tilting your laptop sideways. Watch that signal bar grow. Go for the green! Learn to type sideways! Better yet, redesign your network to extend your range, and always pack a spare external antenna.

Before looking at adding antennas to your network, make sure your card can take an external antenna. Many low-priced cards don't include external connectors anymore. You will have trouble finding a connector to fit the ones that do, as every manufacturer provides its own "proprietary" connector (see Figure 6-6). Check out your friendly local radio supplier for proprietary-to-standard adapters, although they tend to be conveniently overpriced.

Of course, if you have good tools and moderate soldering skills, you may have luck making your own adapter, similar to the one shown in Figure 6-7.

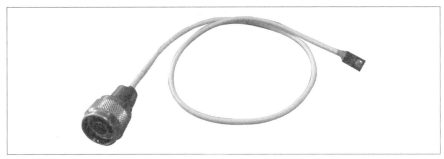

Figure 6-6. The infamous Lucent Pigtail adapter, list price $80

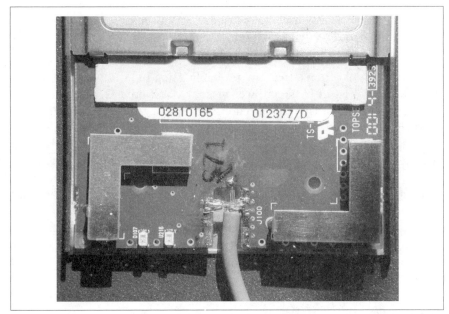

Figure 6-7. A do-it-yourself adapter: $3

The hack-it-in approach is really only practical for a fixed, point-to-point link, as there is no strain relief on the joint. As time marches on, bulk discounts for proprietary-to-standard pigtails are becoming more common. You shouldn't have to spend more than $15–$20 per adapter, particularly if you can buy in quantity. Remember to buy the shortest cable you can use to minimize signal loss in the cable (see the discussion later in this chapter on choosing cable).

Pigtails are manufacturer- (and even model number-) specific, so be sure that you are getting the correct pigtail for the card you intend to use it with. Interesting exceptions to this are the Cisco, Engenius/Senao, and ZCom cards, all of which use an MMCX connector. Also, because PCMCIA cards have limited space for connectors, the pigtail plugs tend to be tiny and *very* fragile. One good tug can ruin your pigtail, connector, or both. You have been warned! (Not that I would personally know how easy they are to break. Not even at 2:00 A.M. after too much espresso and too many hours staring at the video screen, trying to make a deadline. No sir.)

However you attach your antenna to your radio, always look for a way to position your equipment so it can see the antenna at the other end. This is called having *Line of Sight* (*LOS*) to the other node. While it helps on short links (such as from your laptop to your access point), it is absolutely critical on long-distance, point-to-point links. The ideal path between two antennas would be on towers well above any ground clutter, with a valley in between, pointed directly at each other. This is hardly ever the case, but try to get as close to this ideal as possible.

For outdoor applications, trees are probably going to be your single biggest signal killer (followed by metal, wet masonry, and other 2.4GHz gear, not necessarily in that order). When choosing a place to locate your antenna, consider how changes in the environment will affect your link. Remember, what looks like the perfect place in the winter may be completely obscured by leaves in the spring! Walk around the space you have available, and try to find the best possible place for the antenna. Don't just assume that the highest point is the place to install it. After trying every spot on my roof (in vain) to find line of sight to O'Reilly, I got down and sat on my front porch in frustration. It was then that I noticed that I could see the building, about half a mile away, with nothing in between. Setting the antenna on a tripod on my porch, I instantly got a solid signal. Lesson learned: the "right" place for the antenna is different in every installation.

Antennas

Antennas do *not* give you more signal than you started with (that's what amplifiers are for). What they do is focus the available signal in a particular direction, like turning the focus head of a flashlight. It doesn't make the bulb any brighter, it just focuses what you have into a tighter space. Focusing a flashlight gives you a brighter beam that covers a smaller total area, and, likewise, more directional antennas give you a stronger perceived signal in a smaller area. All antennas are somewhat directional, and the measure of their directionality is referred to as *gain*. Typically, the higher the gain, the better the range (in the direction that the antenna radiates best in).

There are four different general types of antennas suitable for 2.4GHz use. Each works well for its own application, and no single antenna works best for every application. Plan ahead of time what your goals are, and configure your network to meet those goals. The following sections describe the most common types of antennas, listed in rough order of increasing directionality.

Omni

Omnidirectional antennas, or omnis (shown in Figure 6-8), radiate outward in all horizontal directions roughly equally. Imagine putting an enormous donut around the center pole of an omni. That is what the radiation pattern looks like. These are good for covering a large area where you don't know which direction your clients might come from. The downside is that they also receive noise from every direction, so they typically aren't as efficient as more directional antennas.

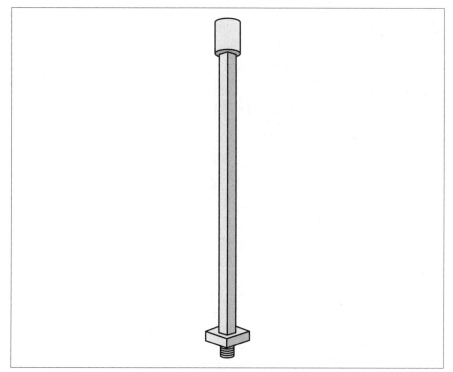

Figure 6-8. Omnis range from tiny extenders to building-mounted poles

They look like tall, thin poles (anywhere from a few inches to several feet long) and tend to be expensive. The longer they are, the more elements they have (and usually more gain, and a higher price). Omni antennas are mounted vertically, like a popsicle stick reaching skyward. They gain in the horizontal, at the expense of the vertical. This means that the worst place to be in relation to an omni is directly beneath (or above) it. The vertical response improves dramatically as you move away from the antenna.

Sector (or sectoral)

Picture an omni with a mirror behind it, and you'll have the radiation pattern of a sector antenna. Sectors radiate best in one direction, with a beam as wide as 180 degrees (or even less). They excel in point-to-multipoint applications, where several clients access the wireless network from the same general direction.

Sector antennas (shown in Figure 6-9) come in a variety of packages, from flattened omnis (tall, thin, and rectangular) to small, flat squares or circles. Some are only eight inches across and mount flat against a vertical wall or on a swivel mount. They can also be ceiling mounted to provide access to a single room, such as a meeting area, classroom, or trade show floor. As with omnis, cost is usually proportional to gain.

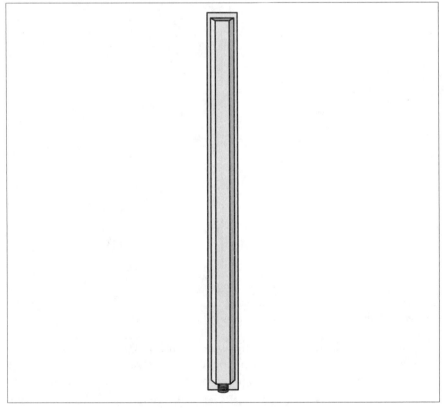

Figure 6-9. Sector antennas tend to be flat and thin

Yagi

A yagi looks like an old television aerial. It is either a flat piece of metal with a bunch of horizontal cross pieces or a long pipe with a bunch of washers along its length (see Figure 6-10). The typical beam width can vary from 15 degrees to as much as 60, depending on the type of antenna. As with omnis, adding more elements means more gain, a longer antenna, and higher cost.

Figure 6-10. Yagis come in various shapes, but all have multiple elements

Some yagis are simply bare, like a flat Christmas tree pointed vaguely in the direction of communications. Others are mounted in long, horizontal PVC cans. They can work well in point-to-point or point-to-multipoint applications, and usually they can achieve higher gain than sectors.

Parabolic dish

In some ways, a dish is the opposite of an omni. Rather than trying to cover the entire area, a dish focuses on a very tight space (see Figure 6-11). Dishes typically have the highest gain and most directionality of any antenna. They are ideal for a point-to-point link, and nearly useless for anything else.

Dishes can be solid or mesh, as small as 18" across or as big as you like (a 30-foot dish is possible, but probably not very convenient). A dish that can send an 802.11b signal more than 20 miles can be as small as a few feet across. In terms of gain for the buck, dishes are probably the cheapest type of antenna. Some people have been successful in converting old satellite and DSS dishes into 2.4GHz dishes; see Chapter 7 for details. Generally speaking, the difference between a mesh reflector and a solid reflector has little to

Figure 6-11. A 24db parabolic dish

do with gain, but when mounting your dish, remember that solid dishes tend to pick up more load from the wind.

Waveguides and "cantennas"

An increasingly popular antenna design is the waveguide. These so-called "cantennas" are easy for home-brew designers to build and offer very high gain for relatively little effort. Waveguides resemble plumbing—they are boxes or cans with nothing in them but a tiny radiator. Figure 6-12 shows an ambitious design made from extruded and milled aluminum.

The Pringles can and coffee can antennas are examples of simple (but effective) home-brew waveguide antennas. I'll describe how to build your own in Chapter 7.

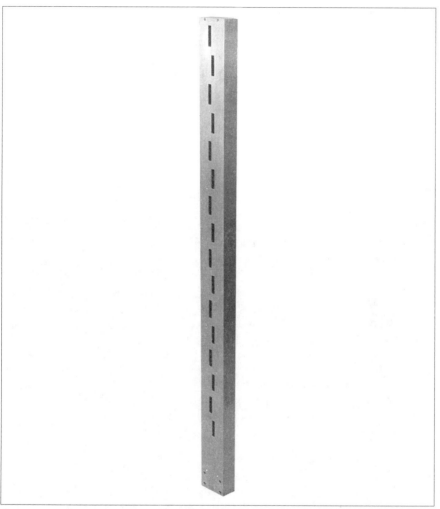

Figure 6-12. A 16dBi, horizontally polarized waveguide that acts like an omni

One other property of antennas worth mentioning here is *polarization*. The polarization of an antenna refers to the direction that the electrical part of the electromagnetic wave travels in. Both horizontal and vertical polarizations are common, but in some exotic antennas, circular (clockwise or counterclockwise) polarization is possible. The polarization of the antenna on each end of a link must match, or the radios will have trouble talking to each other. Omnis and sectors are generally vertically polarized, although horizontally polarized variations do exist. Yagis and dishes can be mounted vertically or horizontally, depending on the application. On a point-to-point link, try both to see which incurs the lowest noise. The polarization of a dish is indicated by the position of the receiving element, not the rear reflector (an oval dish that goes "up and down" is probably mounted in horizontal polarization and, therefore, won't be able to talk very well to a vertically polarized omni).

You can also use polarization to your advantage. For example, you can run two parallel links on the same channel, one with vertical and one with horizontal polarization. If separated by a few feet, two dishes can operate quite happily on the same channel without interfering with each other, and provide twice the bandwidth on the same frequency. This setup would require four antennas, four radios, and Ethernet channel bonding on each end, but is entirely possible.

Cabling

Not all coaxial cable is appropriate for 2.4GHz use. The same piece of cable that delivers high-quality video and audio to your TV is nearly useless for connecting microwave antennas. Choosing the proper type and length of cable is just as important as choosing the right antenna for the job. A 12db sector antenna is useless if you lose 18db in the cable that connects it to the radio. While all cable introduces some loss as signal travels through it, some types of cable do better than others at 2.4GHz.

LMR is a kind of coax cable made by Times Microwave Systems (*http:// www.timesmicrowave.com*) and is possibly the most popular type of cable used for extending 802.11b networks. LMR uses a braided outer shield and solid center conductor, and comes in various sizes.

Heliax is another kind of microwave cabling made by Andrew Corporation (*http://www.andrew.com*). It is made of a semirigid corrugated outer shell (a sort of flexible copper tubing), rather than the braided strands found in coax. The center conductor can be either solid or a corrugated tube inner conductor. It is designed to handle loads *much* greater than (legal) 802.11b installations, it is very expensive, and difficult to work with. It is also extremely low loss. The foam dielectric type part numbers start with LDF.*

In addition to Times Microwave's and Andrew's offerings, Belden, Inc. (*http://www.belden.com*) also makes a very common piece of cable that works well in the 2.4GHz range. You'll frequently see references to 9913; this is Belden 9913.

---

* Don't mess with air dielectric unless you enjoy the challenge of keeping your feed lines pressurized with nitrogen. Air dielectric cable at 802.11b power levels is like the proverbial elephant gun to kill the mosquito.

Generally speaking, the thicker and better-built the cable, the lower the loss and the higher the cost (see Table 6-1). Cable in excess of half an inch or so in thickness is difficult to work with and you may have trouble finding connectors for it. Whenever possible, order the specific length you need, with the proper connectors preinstalled, rather than trying to cut and crimp it yourself. A commercial outlet will usually have the tools and experience needed to make a well-built cable. The best cable in the world won't help you if your connector isn't properly installed.

Table 6-1. Attenuation, size, and approximate cost of microwave coax

Cable type	Diameter	Loss in db/100′ at 2500MHz	Approximate price per foot
LMR-200	0.195"	16.9	$0.37
LMR-400	0.405"	6.8	$0.64
LMR-600	0.509"	4.4	$1.30
LMR-900	0.870"	3.0	$3.70
LMR-1200	1.200"	2.3	$5.50
Belden 9913	0.405"	8.2	$0.97
LDF1-50	0.250"	6.1	$1.66
LDF4-50A	0.500"	3.9	$3.91
LDF5-50A	0.875"	2.3	$2.27
LDF6-50	1.250"	1.7	$10.94
LDF7-50A	1.625"	1.4	$15.76

To sum up: use the best quality cable you can afford, at the shortest length possible. A couple of dB here and there really adds up when dealing with the very low power levels of 802.11b. If you want to put an antenna on the roof, look into weatherproof enclosures for your AP and mount it as close to the antenna as possible. Then run as much Ethernet cable as you need (up to 100 meters!).

Connectors

You have the radio, an antenna, and a length of cable. How do you connect them together? You need to use connectors that work well in the 2.4GHz range, fit the kind of cabling you're using, and mate with each other. Practically all common connectors have two halves, a male and a female (or pin and socket). A few of the more exotic types (such as the APC-7) are sexless, so any connector will match up with any other. Here are the most common connectors you are likely to encounter in the microwave bestiary.

The BNC is a small, cheap connector using a quick-connect half turn (the same connector found on 10base2 Ethernet). The BNC shown in Figure 6-13 isn't well suited for 2.4GHz use, but it is mentioned here because, with the death of 10base2, the connectors are frequently sold for pennies per pound. Don't be tempted.

Figure 6-13. BNC: Bayonet Navy Connector (or Bayonet Neill Concelman, depending on who you ask)

The TNC (see Figure 6-14) is a threaded version of the BNC. The fine threads help eliminate leakage at microwave frequencies. TNCs work well all the way through 12GHz and are usually used with smaller (and higher-loss) cable.

Figure 6-14. TNC (threaded BNC)

An N connector is a larger, threaded connector found on many commercial 2.4GHz antennas (see Figure 6-15). It is larger much than the TNC. It works very well on thicker cable (such as LMR-400) and operates well up to 10GHz. The N is probably the most commonly encountered connector when dealing with 802.11b-compatible gear.

Figure 6-15. N connector

The so-called UHF connector looks like a coarse-thread version of the N (see Figure 6-16). It's not usable for 2.4GHz, but it is sometimes confused with the N. According to the ARRL Microwave manual, it's a PL-259 (which mates with the SO-239 socket). It's not designed to work at microwave frequencies. You should avoid it.

Figure 6-16. The so-called "UHF" connector

The SMA connector (Figure 6-17) is a very popular, small, threaded connector that works great through 18GHz. Their small size precludes using them with large, low-loss cable without using a pigtail.

Figure 6-17. SMA: Sub-Miniature connector, variation A

The SMB (Figure 6-18) is a quick-connect version of the SMC.

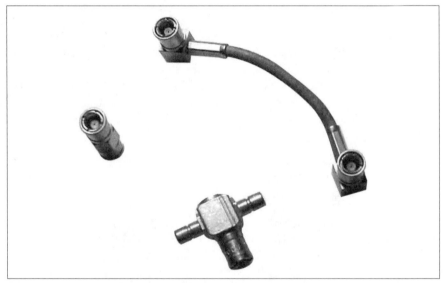

Figure 6-18. SMB: Sub-Miniature connector, variation B

The SMC (see Figure 6-19) is a very small version of the SMA. It is designed to work well through 10GHz, but accepts only *very* small cables.

The APC-7 (see Figure 6-20) is a 7mm sexless connector, usable through 18GHz. It is a high-grade connector manufactured by Amphenol, and it is expensive, fairly rare, and very low loss.

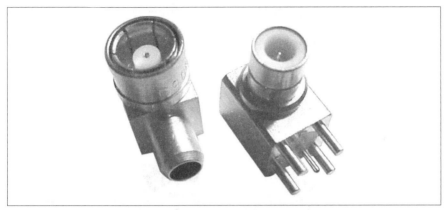

Figure 6-19. SMC: Sub-Miniature connector, variation C (tiny!)

Figure 6-20. APC-7: Amphenol Precision connector, 7mm

Remember that each connector in the system introduces some loss. Avoid adapters and unnecessary connectors whenever possible. Also, commercially built cables tend to be of higher quality than cables you terminate yourself (unless you're really good and have the right tools). Whenever possible, try to buy a pre-made cable with the proper connectors already attached, at the shortest length you can stand. 802.11b gear doesn't put out much power, and every little bit helps extend your range and reliability. It's very easy to make a bad cable, and bad cables can cause no end of trouble.

When matching cables to your equipment, you may encounter connectors of reverse gender (male and female swapped, with same threads), reverse threading (lefthand instead of righthand thread), or even reverse gender reverse threading (both). Make sure you know what you're getting before ordering parts online!

On outdoor installations, proper lightning protection is vital. Gas tube lightning arrestors (shown in Figure 6-21) can provide a high degree of protection (both to your equipment and against fire) from lightning strikes to your antenna. They cost anywhere from $30–$100, and can provide multi-strike protection when properly installed. Most gas tube arrestors I've seen have female N connectors on either end, so be sure to factor that in when considering your hardware installation.

Figure 6-21. A gas tube lightning arrestor

Lightning arrestors won't actually do anything at all unless they are properly grounded. A gas tube is effectively a grounding shunt, making an alternate path for the lightning to travel. Generally, wide copper strap is used to connect to the earth instead of wire, as strap has much lower impedance. Keep your grounding strap as short as possible, and connect it from the gas tube directly to a good grounding rod (no, grounding to the water pipe isn't nearly good enough). If you have more than one antenna, run separate ground straps back to your grounding rod. You want to make it as easy as possible for lightning to find its way back to the earth through your grounding rod, not through your equipment.

There is a wealth of information available online about lightning protection. Check out the following links to get started:

> *http://www.polyphaser.com/ppc_pen_home.asp*
> *http://lightning-protection-institute.com/*

Be sure to read up on proper installation and, when in doubt, call in a professional. It is much cheaper to prevent lightning damage than to clean up after it.

Calculating Range

How far will your signal go? That's a very good question. It depends on all sorts of factors, including the power output and sensitivity of your card, quality of your cable, connectors, and antenna, intervening clutter and noise, and even weather patterns (on long-distance links). While it's impossible to take all of these variables precisely into account, you can make a good estimate before buying any hardware. Here's a simple way to build an estimate (frequently referred to as your *link budget*).

First, figure out how much loss the signal will incur in the space between the two sites. This is called the *path loss*. One common formula for estimating path loss at 2.4GHz is:

$$L = 20 \log(d) + 20 \log(f) + 36.6$$

where L is the loss in dB, d is the distance in miles, and f is the frequency in megahertz.

Suppose you wanted to set up a five-mile link between two points, using channel 6 (2.437GHz):

$$L = 20 \log(5) + 20 \log(2437) + 36.6$$
$$L = (20 * 0.69) + (20 * 3.38) + 36.6$$
$$L = 13.8 + 67.6 + 36.6$$
$$L = 118$$

At five miles, with no obstacles in between, you will lose 118db of signal between the two points. Our link must tolerate that much loss (plus a bit extra to account for weather and miscellaneous interference) or it will be unreliable.

Next, add up all of your gains (radios + antennas + amplifiers) and subtract your losses (cable length, connectors, lightning arrestors, and miscellaneous other losses). Let's assume you are using Orinoco Silver cards (15dBm), no amplifiers, with a 12dBi sector on one side, and a 15dBi yagi on the other. We'll assume you're using one meter of LMR-400 and a lightning arrestor on each side, allowing 0.25dB loss for each connector, and 1dB for each pigtail. Since all of the units are in dB, we can use simple addition and subtraction:

Site A:
Radio − Pigtail − Arrestor − Connector − Cable − Connector + Antenna
  15 − 1 − 1.25 − .25 − .22 − .25 + 12 = 24.03
Plus Site B:
  15 − 1 − 1.25 − .25 − .22 − .25 + 15 = 27.03
Equals: 51.06 total gain

Now subtract the path loss from that total:

  51.06 − 118 = −66.94

This is the perceived signal level at either end of the link: −66.94dBm. But is it enough for communications? Table 6-2 gives the receiver sensitivity specifications for several radio cards.

Table 6-2. Receiver sensitivity matrix for some common radio cards

Radio card	11Mbps	5.5Mbps	2Mbps	1Mbps
Orinoco (Silver or Gold)	−82 dBm	−87 dBm	−91 dBm	−94 dBm
Cisco 340	−83 dBm	−87 dBm	−88 dBm	−90 dBm
Cisco 350	−85 dBm	−89 dBm	−91 dBm	−94 dBm
D-Link DWL-520	−80 dBm	−83 dBm	−86 dBm	−89 dBm
EnGenius / Senao 2511CD	−89 dBm	−91 dBm	−93 dBm	−95 dBm
Linksys WPC11	−76 dBm	−80 dBm	−80 dBm	−80 dBm
Netgear MA101	−84 dBm	−87 dBm	−89 dBm	−91 dBm

The Orinoco Silver card has a receive sensitivity of −82 dBm @ 11Mbps. As we are generating a signal of −66.94dBm, we have a "fudge factor" of 15.06db (82 − 66.94 = 15.06). Theoretically, this will usually work at 11Mbps (in good weather), and should have no problem syncing at 5.5Mbps. The radios should automatically sense when the link becomes unreliable and resync at the fastest possible speed.

Typically, a margin of error of 20db or so is safe enough to account for normal intervening weather patterns. Using more powerful and sensitive radios (such as the Cisco 350 at 20dBm, or the EnGenius/Senao at 23dBm) and higher-gain antennas would help shore up this connection to 11Mbps. Using higher-gain cards in conjunction with high-gain dishes makes it possible to extend your range well beyond 25 miles, but be sure to observe the FCC limits on power and gain. See Tim Pozar's paper in Appendix A for more information.

Online tools such as Green Bay Professional Packet Radio's Wireless Network Link Analysis can give you a good ballpark estimate on what it will take to make your link possible; simply fill in a couple of blanks on a web form. Check out their excellent resources at *http://www.gbonline.com/ ~multiplx/wireless/page09.html*.

If you need radio sensitivity data for a card not included in Table 6-2, look through the documentation provided by your manufacturer. You could also try the table available at *http://www.freenetworks.org/moin/index.cgi/ ReceiveSensitivity*.

Power Amps and the Law

Frequently, when people think of extending range, they immediately think of using amplifiers (I suppose it's only natural; you have an amplifier for your home stereo, why not an amplifier for your network?). Good amplifiers that work in the microwave range have several nontrivial technical obstacles to overcome:

- Amplifiers blindly amplify everything that they're tuned to, both signal and noise. A greater signal won't help you if the noise in the band is increased as well, as the signal will just get lost (like shouting to your friends at a concert).

- 802.11b radio communications are half duplex: they send or receive, but never both at the same time. An amplifier attached to the antenna line must automatically detect when the radio is sending and quickly switch the amp on. When it's finished, it has to quickly cut it off again. Any latency in this switching could actually impair communication or, worse, damage the radio card. Such amplifiers exist, but are not cheap.

- Amplifiers can help a bit on receive by adding some pre-emphasis, but they are really meant for transmitting. This means that if you have an amp only on one end of a link, the other end may be able to hear you, but you may not hear them. To make amps effective, you'll need them on both ends of the link.

- All amplifiers require power to operate. This means adding a DC injector to your antenna feed line or using an external adapter. This further drives up the cost of your node and makes yet another device that you have to provide power for.

As a result, amplifiers that work well with 802.11b gear are expensive ($400+) and difficult to come by. But do you really need them? Using standard gear and high-gain antennas, you can extend a point-to-point link to 25+ miles, without amplifiers. Your money is probably better spent on high-quality directional antennas and cabling, and possibly even adding another node for further saturation.

As far as U.S. federal law is concerned, you'll have to read Part 15 and draw your own conclusions. Hire a lawyer if you're really paranoid. BAWUG member Tim Pozar has put together an excellent paper on interpreting the Part 15 rules; see Appendix A for his excellent work.

In short, the amount of power you can legally run (and the gain of your antenna) is limited, depending on how you use it. Fixed point-to-point links are allotted the most power, while omnidirectional point-to-multipoint configurations are the most restricted. Unless you use amplifiers, you aren't likely to run into the FCC limits, because standard client cards don't put out nearly enough power. But don't just take my word for it, because I am not a lawyer. (Besides, the person responsible for making sure that your rig is legal is you, the operator!)

I do believe that the intent behind the rules is to limit interference in the band, which is something we should all fight to make happen. Noise is everyone's enemy. To that end, try to use the least amount of power necessary to keep your link going, and use the most directional antennas that will work for your application. Be a good neighbor, and you may find that you enjoy your neighborhood more.

## CHAPTER 7

Other Applications

Thanks to the efforts of countless engineers, we have an open 802.11b standard. Now that hardware that adheres to this standard is in the hands of non-engineers, all sorts of interesting applications have been implemented. Thousands around the globe are pushing the capabilities of these inexpensive radios well beyond their intended limits. Standard client PCMCIA cards have been used to create point-to-point backbone links several miles apart. Discontent with tiny, private networks, people are using inexpensive access points to create public networks that can support hundreds of simultaneous users. Even the popularized security shortcomings of 802.11b are being overcome by some careful planning and the proper application of open source software. Whether the IEEE committee intended it to be so or not, 802.11b has stumbled on the magic formula that makes the ultimate platform for hardware hackery: low cost, ease of use, ease of modification, and ubiquity.

In this chapter, we'll take a look at some wireless applications that demonstrate the enormous flexibility of wireless (and some that are just really cool!). Be warned that some of these examples will certainly void warranties and may damage your equipment if you're not careful. If you are ever unsure about how to proceed, ask around. Chances are, someone else has done what you're thinking of doing, and can at least lend you their shared experience. The various wireless group mailing lists are a great resource for ideas and working out implementation details.

Software

While client software drivers are a good starting point, there are a number of free (or nearly free) utilities that will assist you with site surveys and link analysis. Here are some of the most popular 802.11b network tools today.

NetStumbler *http://www.netstumbler.com/*

By far the most popular wireless discovery tool on the planet, NetStumbler provides a wealth of information about available networks. It will show you ESSIDs, AP MAC addresses, channels, WEP status, and more. It can show the relative signal and noise of a particular AP, making it handy for setting up point-to-point shots. It is only available for Windows.

MacStumbler *http://www.macstumbler.com/*

This is a beta version of a NetStumbler-like application for Mac OS X. Like its Windows counterpart, it shows all available networks and the channels they are using. While it does a fair job of network discovery, currently it isn't particularly useful for setting up point-to-point shots, as it doesn't display a high-resolution signal strength meter.

Kismac *http://www.binaervarianz.de/projekte/programmieren/kismac/*

Kismac is another Mac OS X application that uses the RF Monitor mode of the AirPort and Prism 2 cards to observe networks. It also allows the user to send raw frames to any AP or client and has a handy real-time graph of available networks and their relative usage.

Wavemon *http://www.wavemage.com/projects.html*

Wavemon is an excellent ncurses-based network monitor for Linux. It has a number of useful features, including real-time signal and noise levels, an AP scanner, and a full-screen moving histogram. This helps tremendously when trying to find the other end of a long-distance link.

Kismet *http://www.kismetwireless.net/*

If you're looking for an exceptional raw RF monitor, look no further. Kismet can find APs (including APs running a closed network), send and receive raw frames, and even detect the presence of people running NetStumbler. Its sophisticated data logger allows export of raw 802.11 frames to tools such as *tcpdump* and Ethereal for later analysis. It currently runs only on Linux but versions for Linux-ARM, BSD, Windows, and OS X are under development.

These tools, combined with a good network analysis package (such as Ethereal), can help you find out a tremendous amount of information about how wireless networks in your area are being used. Keep them with you on site surveys, and you'll be able to do a much better job of planning your network.

Point-to-Point Links

From a radio perspective, point-to-point links are very straightforward to set up. You should always follow more or less the same steps when evaluating the possibility of a link:

- Establish that you have line of sight from end to end.
- Measure the distance between the points and calculate the path loss.
- Add in the capabilities of your equipment to determine your link budget.
- Go out and hook up your gear.

If you intend to make a long-distance point-to-point link, first find out the latitude, longitude, and altitude of each end point. You can find this by physically going to each site and marking the coordinates with a GPS, or you can estimate using topographical maps or software (see Chapter 6 for some examples of how to do this). With the coordinates and altitude of both sites, you can calculate a bearing and tilt angle, so you know roughly where to point the antennas on each end. A decent GPS can help here by giving you a bearing to and from each point. You should also check out the online wireless design CGIs at *http://www.gbonline.com/~multiplx/wireless/page09.html* for help with many of the calculations you'll need to perform.

Obviously, if you can see the other point through binoculars or a telescope, this is a good first step. Ideally, there should be very little on the ground between the two points. The closer the path is to an actual valley, the better. Take a look at Chapter 6 for details about how to calculate the path loss and link budget for your link. I've mentioned it before, but here it is again: keep your antenna cable as short as possible! On a long-distance point-to-point link, every few decibels count.

Now that you're ready to hook up your gear, the question remains: what gear do you want to use? That depends on your (fiscal) budget and how you plan to use the link. As we saw in Chapter 5, it is very simple to set up a Linux gateway in IBSS or Host AP mode. This is a popular and flexible way to go, but setup can be a little complex if it's your first link. If you already have a hardware access point, you can use it for one end of the link, and have a computer using a client card on the other. Another alternative is to use an access point that will bridge over the air, such as the Linksys WAP11 (although there are varying reports of success and stability with that particular model). Keeping your WAP11 firmware up to date seems to be the best move you can make toward greater operating stability. Finally, it is also possible to use client hardware (such as the Orinoco Ethernet Converter or Linksys WET11) on one end of the link to talk to an access point on the other end. People have had different experiences with these devices, but, generally speaking, firmware updates seem to resolve most issues.

The farther apart your points are, the harder it will be to aim your antennas. At distances up to five miles or so, this is rarely a problem (as long as you have enough total gain to overcome the path loss). At greater distances, getting the antennas pointed directly at each other can be quite tricky. Here are some techniques that might help you get your dishes pointed in the right direction:

- Use cell phones or radios to maintain communications between the two points while you're aiming the antennas. It helps to have at least two people at each end (one to manipulate the antenna, and another to coordinate with the other end).

- Set up all your network settings ahead of time, so there aren't any variables once you get to the remote site. Check all gear, ping each box, and even transfer a file or two to be sure that your equipment works at close range. You don't want to question it later if you have problems getting the link going.

- Use a tool such as the Lucent Link Test meter (which ships with the Windows driver for the Orinoco card) or any of the other tools mentioned earlier in this chapter to show the signal strength and noise readings in real time. This kind of tool is your best friend, short of an actual spectrum analyzer.

- Work on one end of the link at a time, slowly changing one variable at a time until you see the maximum signal strength and lowest noise at each end of the link.

- If you have one handy (and your link budget permits it), first try an omni or sector antenna on one end of the link. Once you find the other end of the link, replace it with your dish or yagi, and tune it in.

- Sweep slowly, and don't be afraid to go beyond the best perceived signal. Most antennas have smaller side lobes that appear as a false positive. Keep moving until you find the main lobe. It should stand out significantly from the others, once you find it.

- Do *not* touch the actual antenna when taking a reading. This is particularly easy to overlook when using tube yagis, like the Pringles can (see the later section). Resting your hand on the antenna tube will interfere with the radiation pattern and drain your signal very quickly. Take your readings with all hands clear of the equipment.

- Don't forget to compare horizontal and vertical polarization. Try the antennas in both positions, and use the one that shows the lowest noise (see the section "Redundant Links" later in this chapter).
- Once your link is in place, consider using WEP to discourage others from attempting to connect to it. If you want to provide wireless access at either end-point, set up another gateway, preferably with caching services (such as caching DNS and a transparent web proxy, like Squid). This helps reduce the amount of traffic that goes over the long link, helps cut down on network collisions, and generally makes more efficient use of the link.

It can take all day to properly align antennas at a great distance, but it can also be a fun time with the right group of people. Just take your time, think about what you're doing, and be sure to leave time at the end of the day to celebrate!

There is something I must mention here: I know you're probably excited about getting your link up and running, but never neglect attention to safety. Mounting antennas on roofs or poles can be hazardous, particularly if you are preoccupied by thoughts of link budgets, pigtails, and signal strength meters. In February of 2002, I nearly lost my own life when I fell from a friend's roof while working on a point-to-point link. I had been on many, many roofs at that point, and carelessly went out on a roof after sunset. I remember thinking, "It's getting dark, but we're almost done. I'll just go out and finish up." In the next minute, I stepped off of the roofline and ended up in a hospital for the next week (and recovering over the next several months).

When working on a wireless project, take your time, make sure you have plenty of light, and always work with a friend if you're doing anything precarious. Pay attention to power lines. Whenever possible, you should wear a harness when working on a roof or other high place. Remember that the problem will always be there for you to solve…tomorrow. Building your own network is tremendously rewarding, but no link is worth risking your life.

Point-to-Multipoint Links

Setting up a point-to-multipoint configuration is much like setting up a point-to-point link with an access point. The difference is that multiple clients connect to a single AP. You can use any sort of antenna, but you should generally choose one with the narrowest beam width that will cover the area you're interested in. That helps reject noise from all other directions, and minimizes the noise that your network will cause for other people.

You should pay particular attention to the "hidden node" problem when dealing with long-distance point-to-multipoint links. On a simple point-to-point shot, this isn't a problem, because both nodes can hear each other by definition. But suppose you put an access point on a high point and attach a high-gain omnidirectional antenna to it, thus allowing multiple clients to connect. It is very likely that some clients may not be able to hear the traffic of others, so transmission collisions will occur. An increase in traffic passing through your AP can bring down throughput considerably.

One common method for dealing with long-distance point-to-multipoint collisions is to sectorize your AP: that is, add multiple radios attached to tight beam sector (or other) antennas to your AP site. Setting each antenna to a different channel and making intelligent use of polarization tricks can help reduce the number of clients associated with each AP, which reduces the problem of collisions.

If your AP supports it, you can also use RTS/CTS (Request To Send/Clear to Send). Using RTS/CTS guarantees that clients do not transmit simultaneously—each frame must first be approved for transmission, then acknowledged by the access point. Unfortunately, there is considerable overhead involved with RTS/CTS, so it is usually left off by default. If your AP is in a prominent place and shows many receive errors, consider trying RTS/CTS. Run a throughput test while the network is under typical load without using RTS/CTS, then turn it on and try again. The error rate should go down considerably on your AP, but your throughput may suffer. Fine-tuning RTS/CTS can be difficult—since 802.11b gear has become cheaper, it is frequently more effective to simply add more equipment to accommodate more clients.

Home-Brew Antennas

Since the first edition of this book was published, many new home-brew antenna designs that work at 2.4GHz have been published online (and more are being thought up every day). Here are just two ingenious examples.

The Pringles Can

At the Portland Summit in June 2001, Andrew Clapp (*http://www.netscum. com/~clapp/*) presented a novel yagi antenna design. It used a bolt, metal tubing, washers, and PVC tubing to make an inexpensive "shotgun" yagi, either 18" or 36" long. While his antenna shows between 12 and 15dBi gain (which is impressive for such a simple design), it's also quite large. When we returned from Portland, some members of our local group and I realized that, if we were careful, we could fit a full wavelength inside of a Pringles can as shown in Figure 7-1. This would show a reduced total gain, but it would also make the entire antenna much more compact.

Figure 7-1. The complete antenna (it's just a can!)

Parts list:

Part	Approximate cost
All-thread, 5 5/8" long, 1/8" OD	$1.00
Two nylon lock nuts	$0.10
Five 1" washers, 1/8" ID	$0.10
6" aluminum tubing, 1/4" ID	$0.75
A connector to match your radio pigtail (we used a female N connector)	$3.00
1 1/2" piece of 12 gauge solid copper wire (we used ground wire from house electrical wiring)	negligible
A tall Pringles can (any flavor, Ridges are optional)	$1.50
Scrap plastic disc, 3" across (like another Pringles can lid)	negligible
Total:	$6.45

Of course, buying in bulk helps a lot. You probably won't be able to find a 6-inch piece of all-thread; buy the standard size (usually one or two feet) and a 10-pack of washers and nuts while you're at it. Then you'll have more than enough parts to make two, all for about $10.

Required tools

You'll need the following tools to make your antenna:

- Ruler
- Scissors
- Pipe cutter (or hacksaw or dremel tool, in a pinch)
- Heavy-duty cutters (or dremel again, to cut the all-thread)
- Something sharp to pierce the plastic (an awl or a drill bit will work)
- Hot glue gun (unless you have a screw-down type connector)
- Soldering iron

Construction time should be about an hour.

Front collector construction

Mark and cut four pieces of tubing, about 1.2 inches (1 15/64 inches). Where did I get this number? First, figure out the wavelength at the bottom of the frequency range we're using (2.412GHz, or channel 1). This will be the longest that the pipe should be:

$$W = 3.0 \times 10^8 \times (1 / 2.412) \times 10^{-9}$$
$$W = (3.0 / 2.412) \times 10^{-1}$$
$$W = 0.124 \text{ meters}$$
$$W = 4.88 \text{ inches}$$

We'll be cutting the pipe to quarter wavelength, so:

$$^1/4 \, W = 4.88 / 4$$
$$^1/4 \, W = 1.22 \text{ inches}$$

Now figure out what the shortest length we'll ever use is (2.462GHz, or channel 11 in the United States):

$$W = 3.0 \times 10^8 \times (1 / 2.462) \times 10^{-9}$$
$$W = (3.0 / 2.462) \times 10^{-1}$$
$$W = 0.122 \text{ meters}$$
$$W = 4.80 \text{ inches}$$
$$1/4 \, W = 1.20 \text{ inches}$$

Practically speaking, what's the difference between the shortest pipe and the longest pipe length? About 0.02 inches, or less than 1/32 of an inch. That's probably about the size of the pipe cutter blade you're using. So, just shoot for 1.2 inches, and you'll get it close enough.

Cut the all-thread to exactly 5 5/8 inches. The washers we used are about 1/16 of an inch thick, so that should leave just enough room for the pipe, washers, and nuts.

Pierce a hole in the center of the Pringles can lid big enough for the all-thread to pass through. Now is probably a good time to start eating Pringles (we found it better for all concerned to just toss the things; salt and vinegar-flavored Pringles are almost caustic after the first fifteen or so. Heed the recommended serving size!).

Cut a 3-inch plastic disc just big enough to fit snugly inside the can. We found that another Pringles lid, with the outer ridge trimmed off, works just fine. Poke a hole in the center of it, and slip it over one of the lengths of pipe.

Now, assemble the pipe. You might have to use a file or dremel tool to shave the tips of the thread if you have trouble getting the nuts on. The pipe is a sandwich that goes on the all-thread as shown in Figure 7-2.

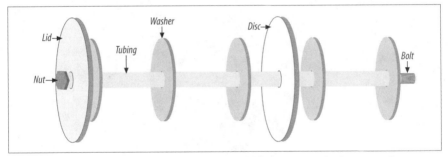

Figure 7-2. Nut, lid, washer, pipe, washer, pipe, washer, pipe-with-plastic, washer, pipe, washer, nut

Tighten down the nuts to be snug, but don't overtighten (I bent the tubing on our first try; aluminum bends *very* easily). Just get it snug. Congratulations, you now you have a front collector just like the one shown in Figure 7-2.

Preparing the can

By now you should have eaten (or tossed) the actual chips. Wipe out the can, and measure 3 3/8 inches up from the bottom of the can. Cut a hole just big enough for the connector to pass through. We found through trial and error that this seems to be the "sweet spot" of the can. On our Pringles Salt & Vinegar can, the N connector sat directly between "Sodium" and "Protein."

Element construction

Straighten the heavy copper wire and solder it to the connector. When inside the can, the wire should be just below the midpoint of the can (ours turned out to be about 1 1/16 inches). You lose a few dB by going longer, so cut it just shy of the middle of the can.

We were in a hurry, so we used hot glue to hold the connector in place on our first antenna. If you have a connector that uses a nut and washer, and you're really careful about cutting the hole, these work very well (and aren't nearly as messy as hot glue). Just remember that you're screwing into cardboard when you connect your pigtail. It's very easy to forget and accidentally tear the wall of the can.

Now, insert the collector assembly into the can and close the lid. The inside end of the pipe should *not* touch the copper element; it should be just forward of it. If it touches, your all-thread is probably too long. Figure 7-3 shows a completed antenna.

Figure 7-3. The completed antenna

How can you estimate gain without access to high-end radio analysis gear? Use the Link Test software that comes with the Orinoco silver cards to read the signal and noise readings (in dB) at both ends of a connection. As I happen to live six-tenths of a mile (with clean line of sight) from O'Reilly headquarters, we had a fairly controlled testbed to experiment with. We shot at the omni on the roof and used the access point at O'Reilly as our link test partner.

To estimate antenna performance, we started by connecting commercial antennas of known gain and taking readings. Then we connected our test antennas and compared the results. We had the following at our disposal:

- Two 10dBi, 180-degree sector panel antennas
- One 11dBi, 120-degree sector panel antenna
- One 24dBi parabolic dish
- A couple of Pringles cans and some hardware

Here were the average received signal and noise readings from each, in approximately the same physical position:

Antenna	Signal	Noise
10dBi A	−83db	−92db
10dBi B	−83db	−92db
11dBi	−82db	−95db
24dBi	−67db	−102db
Pringles can	−81db	−98db

The test partner (AP side) signal results were virtually the same. Interestingly, even at only six-tenths of a mile, we saw some thermal fade effect; as the evening turned into night, we saw about 3db gain across the board. (It had been a particularly hot day: almost 100 degrees. I don't know what the relative humidity was, but it felt fairly dry.)

Yagis and dishes are much more directional than sectors and omnis. This bore out in the numbers, as the perceived noise level was consistently lower with the more directional antennas. This can help a lot on long-distance shots; not only will your perceived signal be greater, the competing noise will seem to be less. More directional antennas also help keep noise down for any neighbors who might be trying to share the spectrum. Be a good neighbor and use the most directional antennas that will work for your application (yes, noise is everybody's problem).

The Pringles can seemed to have large side lobes that extend about 45 degrees from the center of the can. Don't point the can directly at where you're trying to go; aim slightly to the left or the right. We also found that elevating the antenna helped a bit. When aiming the antenna, hold it behind the connector, and *slowly* sweep from left to right, with the Link Test program running. When you get the maximum signal, slowly raise the end of the can to see if it makes a difference. Go slowly, changing only one variable at a time.

Remember that the can is polarized, so match the phase of the antenna you're talking to. For example, if shooting at an omni, be sure the element is on the bottom or the top of the can, or you won't be able to see it! See the earlier discussion on antenna polarization for how you can use this effect to your advantage.

We were fortunate enough to have a member of our community group bring a return loss meter to one of our meetings, and we were able to get some actual measurements of how much signal was returning to the radio. The results weren't as good as I had hoped, but they showed that the antenna was usable, particularly at lower frequencies. Most likely, failing to take into account the thickness of the washers has made the entire front element a little too long. There isn't nearly enough power leaving the radio to cause damage due to high return loss, but it does point out that the antenna isn't as well tuned as it could be.

Stew and Cookie Cans

Since the Pringles can story was published, I have received a phenomenal amount of email from people who have tried it for themselves. While some people simply enjoyed making a recycled antenna out of a piece of trash, many others wrote to say, "You know, that's not a bad design, but some friends and I found a better way to do it…" One such person was Gregory Rehm. He took my Pringles can design and another coffee can design that I was working on, and pitted them against his own designs (including a 40-ounce stew can) in a Wireless Shootout Battle Royale. His experimentation and excellent analysis is documented on his web site at *http://www. turnpoint.net/wireless/has.html*. It is very entertaining to read, but in case you're too filled with suspense to operate a browser: his stew can won by a mile.

As it turns out, it is much simpler to make a tin can waveguide antenna than to bother with cutting pipe and spacing washers apart on all-thread. Gregory has an excellent how-to (complete with photos, diagrams, and formulae) online at *http://www.turnpoint.net/wireless/cantennahowto.html*.

Another common can that approaches the ideal size for 2.4GHz is the Pepperidge Farm Pirouette can (see Figure 7-4). It makes a much simpler, sturdier, and more efficient antenna than a Pringles can, and you get to eat the cookies!

Figure 7-4. The Pirouette cantenna

There are a number of variations on the basic waveguide antenna floating around the Internet, involving such wacky ideas as modified DSS dishes and sardine cans. Look at any of the major wireless community sites for a variety of antenna designs, including omnis, yagis, waveguides, and much more.

Redundant Links

All antennas show a characteristic known as polarity, which refers to the direction that the electrical field moves in as it leaves the antenna. Simultaneously, magnetic waves leave the antenna at a 90-degree angle to the electrical waves. Most common antennas show a linear polarity (i.e., vertical or horizontal). Some antennas, like a wound helical antenna,* actually demonstrate circular polarity, in which the waves move outward in a spiral, always perpendicular to each other.

In order for one antenna to receive the signals of another, the polarity must match. Omnidirectionals (and most sectors) have vertical polarity. Dishes and yagis can be mounted vertically, horizontally, or somewhere in between. The Pringles can is just a yagi, and its polarity is determined by the position of the antenna connector. A circularly polarized antenna (like the helical) has its polarity determined by the direction of the outer winding: either clockwise or counterclockwise.

You can use polarity to your advantage to try to eliminate some noise on a long-distance link. First try each end in vertical polarization and measure the perceived noise. Then rotate each end 90 degrees and measure the noise again. Use the position that shows the least amount of noise, and you should have a more stable link. Figure 7-5 shows typical polarization.

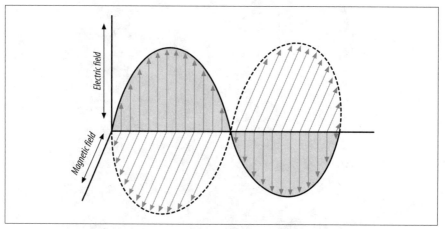

Figure 7-5. The polarization of an antenna is determined by the direction of its electrical field; the magnetic field is perpendicular to the electrical field

Since an antenna can receive signals only from antennas whose polarity matches its own, you can also use this property to make more efficient

---

* See *http://users.bigpond.net.au/jhecker/* for details and plans for this interesting design!

redundant links. For example, suppose you wanted to use two radios at either end of a link to provide 22Mbps total bandwidth to a remote location. Usually, you would need to use two channels separated by 25MHz (i.e., 1 and 6, or 2 and 7, or 3 and 8). If you use one antenna with vertical polarization and another with horizontal polarization, and separate the antennas by a few feet, you could use the same channel for all of your traffic. This means less noise in the band for you and your neighbors (and it theoretically gives you up to six possible simultaneous links without interference, where normally only three were possible).

As far as IP goes, you can either route the traffic independently or use the channel bonding features of the Linux 2.4 kernel to weld all of your connections into one big pipe. This mode of operations is new, experimental, and left as an exercise to the reader (hey, if you're anything like me, you could stand more exercise in your life).

Repeaters

Unfortunately, long-distance line of sight isn't always possible. Sometimes, you will encounter an obstacle that you simply can't go over (or through). Or you might need to stretch a link to go farther than your available radios and antennas permit. Maybe you are just on the edge of range of a good AP, but need to provide access to a room full of people (and they don't all have high-gain antennas). A repeater may help in your application.

A radio repeater is a piece of equipment with two complete radios in it. Any traffic heard on the first radio is repeated to the second, and vice versa. If directional antennas are used, a weak signal reaching one of the transmitters is then rebroadcast over the other channel, as if it had originated from that point. Figure 7-6 shows the use of this technique to extend range or get around obstacles.

While a classic radio repeater might work fine with 802.11b, I unfortunately don't have access to radio gear capable of broadcasting a 25MHz wide signal at 2.4GHz. But I do have the next best thing: a couple of 802.11b PCMCIA cards.

The following sections describe three repeater-like configurations that are useful in many circumstances.

Two Cards in One PC

If you have a PC with two PCMCIA slots, you can configure Linux to use both interfaces and pass packets between them. Insert two wireless cards,

Figure 7-6. A repeater does just that: repeat everything it hears to someone else down the line

and you have the hardware needed for a repeater application. While many client cards specifically disable Ethernet bridging, you can still use masquerading between the interfaces to bring two networks together.

One intriguing portable device that works well as a repeater is the Fujitsu Stylistic 1000. It is an old 486/100 tablet PC that comes with a monochrome LCD screen, stylus, 200MB PCMCIA hard drive, no keyboard, all of the usual PC ports, a lithium ion battery, and two extra PCMCIA slots. You can pick them up through used parts suppliers for around $100. (Thanks to the BAWUG crew for finding these nifty little devices!)

Take a look at Chapter 5 for details on how to get Linux installed and configured for masquerading. Once the software is configured, the only remaining issue is: how do you squeeze one card on top of the other? Most wireless cards have a slight protruding bulge to make room for their internal antenna and won't fit in a stacked PCMCIA bay.

There are a couple of ways around this problem. Obviously, if you're using a card like the Cisco LMC35x or Senao 2511 for the bottom card, there is no bulge and therefore no problem. If you're using a card like the D-Link DWL-650,* the bulge is small enough that you can just squeeze two cards in at the same time. If you're using an Orinoco card on the bottom, your only recourse is to pop the plastic cover off and remove the two silver internal antenna tabs. This will make the card more or less useless without an external antenna, but can be worth it if you're pressed for time (or cash) and have

---

* See *http://kevlar.burdell.org/~will/antenna/* for one quick way to add an external antenna to the DWL-650.

a card that you're willing to dedicate to long-distance work. Remember to connect an external antenna to both radios when using two in one machine, or else the transmitters will be operating right next to each other, causing a tremendous amount of interference.

This technique, shown in Figure 7-7, is very inexpensive, but it isn't exactly ideal. Even setting the radios to different channels doesn't help eliminate all of the interference, as the transmitters are simply too close together (it will work fine on lightly loaded networks, but won't stand up to a large amount of constant traffic). To be able to take full advantage of using two radios in a repeater, you'll need to separate them slightly, which is much easier to do in a desktop PC.

Figure 7-7. Two Orinoco cards in one Stylistic—a snug fit

Two APs Back-to-Back

Many access points are capable of bridging the wireless network directly to the wire. What happens if you connect two APs in bridging mode back-to-back over a crossover CAT5 cable? Naturally, you have a bridging repeater.

I have only tried this with two Apple AirPorts, shown in Figure 7-8, but theoretically any AP capable of bridge mode should work fine. In this configuration, anyone within range of access point A will have their traffic repeated verbatim to access point B, and vice versa. As the Apple AirPorts actually use Orinoco Silver radio cards, the necessary external antenna connectors are already present inside the UFO. In fact, by removing the outer shell, it is possible to mount both AirPorts in a single, small, weatherproof box, with each connected to its own directional antenna. Each AirPort can even be configured with its own channel and security settings, if necessary. Performance won't be as optimal as with a straight shot (because you have doubled your chances of a data collision), but it can make a connection possible where one might otherwise be impossible.

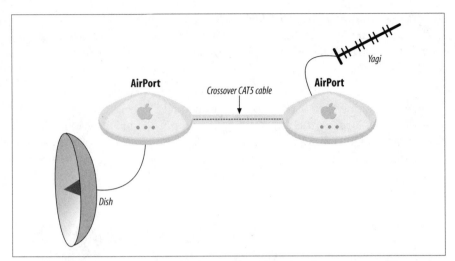

Figure 7-8. Two Apple Airports in bridge mode, connected with a crossover cable, can act as an 802.11b repeater

With the advent of client devices (such as the Linksys WET11), it is also possible to extend your network by using such a device directly connected to an AP in bridge mode. Set the client adapter to the ESSID of the network you want to link to, then set the bridged AP to a different ESSID, and away you go. Be sure to use the latest firmware on the WET11 before trying this; early models had severe problems (specifically, with MAC table overruns) that were fixed in later revisions.

Advanced Host AP Modes

Wireless Distribution System (WDS) is part of the 802.11b standard. It is designed to allow APs to talk to each other over the air and to bridge two attached networks together. Unfortunately, access points that implement interoperable WDS are rare, and AP to AP bridges tend to be manufacturer-specific. The Host AP driver discussed in Chapter 5 has the beginnings of an interesting WDS implementation that allows the host to simultaneously serve as a WDS bridge and a standard AP. Unfortunately, due to limitations in the Prism 2 firmware, true WDS isn't yet achievable, but a WDS-like mode is still possible through a clever protocol hack. This allows machines running Host AP to talk to each other over the air and serve local clients at the same time, potentially allowing for rapid expansion of wireless networks.

Another interesting bit of code just appearing in the Host AP CVS tree is the possibility of running as a BSS master and BSS client at the same time—as

---

long as both operate on the same channel. This performs the same function as a working WDS implementation, but could theoretically work with any access point (even APs that don't support WDS). This code is very experimental at this stage, but it looks promising. Keep an eye on the Host AP development if you are interested in pushing the limits of what is possible with access point technology.

Security Concerns

When using an open wireless network, all traffic between your laptop and the access point is sent in the clear to anyone in range. When using WEP, anyone who shares the same WEP key can listen in on your traffic as if it were an open network. How can you protect your data from prying eyes while using wireless? The best possible protection is provided by end-to-end encryption, which is provided by tools such as SSL, PPTP, and SSH. For example, browsing to an SSL-enabled web page will keep your conversation private, leaving any would-be eavesdroppers with data that looks much like line noise. The encryption and identification facilities provided by the 128-bit SSL implementation is widely regarded as "good enough" for use over untrusted networks, both wired and wireless.

SSL may be fine for web pages (and some mail clients), but what about protecting other traffic? The following is one method for securing your email using OpenSSH.* For a more thorough exploration of the possibilities of SSH, I highly recommend *SSH, The Secure Shell: The Definitive Guide* (O'Reilly).

OpenSSH is being developed for BSD, but thanks to the great work by their porting team, it compiles under many Unix-like operating systems (including Linux, Solaris, HP/UX, Mac OS X, and many others). You can even use it in Windows with the Cygwin package (check out *http://www.cygwin.com* and download it now, if you haven't already; it almost makes Windows fun to use!).

Download OpenSSH and build it. You'll also need a copy of the OpenSSL libraries to compile OpenSSH. You can get OpenSSL from *http://www. openssl.org*. Once you've installed OpenSSH, you can use it to tunnel POP traffic from your local laptop to your mail server (called "mailhost"). We'll assume you have a shell account on the mail server for this example, although any machine on your internal network that accepts SSH connections should suffice.

---

* OpenSSH (*http://www.openssh.com*) is a free, open source implementation of the SSH protocol.

Establish the Connection

Under OpenSSH:

```
laptop# ssh -L 110:mailhost:110 -l user -N mailhost
```

Naturally, substitute *user* with your username, and *mailhost* with your mail server's hostname or IP address. Note that you will have to be root on your laptop for this example, since you'll be binding to a privileged port (110, the POP port). You should also disable any locally running POP daemon (look in */etc/inetd.conf*), or it will get in the way.

Assuming you have your RSA or DSA keys set up, you can even run this in the background (just tack on an &). This sets up the tunnel, and starts forwarding your local ports to the remote end through it. The -N switch tells SSH to not bother running an actual command on the remote end and to just do the forwarding.

Configure Your Mail Software

You now need to tell your mail software to connect to your tunnel rather than connecting directly to your mail server. This is different in each application, but the idea is always the same: you want your email client to connect to *localhost* instead of *mailhost*.

Here's how to set it up under Netscape Communicator; other clients may have different menu choices, but the principle is the same:

- Go to Edit → Preferences.
- Expand the Mail & Newsgroups tree, and select Mail Servers.
- Remove your existing incoming mail server, and add a new one.
- Under General, type "localhost" as the Server Name. Select POP3 as the Server Type.
- Hit OK, make sure your tunnel is established, and retrieve your mail.

Naturally, it doesn't have to end with POP. You can also forward SMTP for outgoing mail (port 25). Simply specify multiple -L entries, like this:

```
laptop# ssh -L 110:mailhost:110 -L 25:mailhost:25 -l user -N mailhost
```

Now just set your outgoing mail server to *localhost*, and all of your incoming and outgoing email will be protected from prying eyes (er, ears) on your wireless network.

NoCatAuth Captive Portal

While some node owners are perfectly happy opening their networks to whomever happens to be in range, most of us hesitate at the thought of paying for our neighbors to use our bandwidth. After all, apart from using up resources that we're paying for, anonymous users could potentially abuse other networks and have their shenanigans traced back to our network! If we want to provide responsible wireless access, we need a way to securely identify users when they connect and then allocate only the resources that the node owner is willing to contribute. After the Portland Summit, it was obvious that one key component was missing from the community network idea: a freely available *captive portal* implementation.

The idea behind a captive portal is fairly straightforward. Rather than relying on the built-in security features of 802.11b to control who can associate with an AP, we configure the access point with no WEP and as an open network. The AP is also in bridged mode and connected via a crossover cable to an Ethernet card on a Linux router. It is then up to the router to issue DHCP leases, throttle bandwidth, and permit access to other networks. When a user attempts to browse any web page, they are redirected to a page that presents the user with a login prompt and information about the node they are connected to. If the wireless gateway has a method of contacting a central authority to determine the identity of the connected wireless user, then it can relax its firewall rules appropriately and allow the privileges due to that user (for example, more bandwidth or access to other machines and ports).

The *NoCatAuth* project implements such a third-party authentication system (or Auth system, for short). Written in Perl and C, it takes care of presenting the user with a login prompt, contacts a MySQL database to look up user credentials, securely notifies the wireless gateway of the user's status, and authorizes further access. On the gateway side, the software manages local connections, sets bandwidth throttling and firewall rules, and times out old logins after a user-specified time limit. The software is released under the GPL (*http://www.gnu.org/copyleft/gpl.html*).

We are designing the system so that trust is ultimately preserved; the gateways and end users need only trust the Auth system, which is secured with a registered SSL certificate. Passwords are never given to the wireless gateway (thus protecting the users from "bad guy" node owners), and gateway rules are modified only by a cryptographically signed message from the Auth system (protecting the gateway from users or upstream sites trying to spoof the Auth system).

We provide for three possible classes of wireless user:

- Public Class
- Co-op Class
- Owner Class

A typical *Public Class* user knows nothing about the local wireless group, and simply is looking for access to the Internet. This class is granted very little bandwidth, and users are restricted in what services they can access by the use of firewall rules. The Public Class of user is given the opportunity to learn more about who is providing the wireless service and how they can get in touch with the local group (and ultimately get more access). They do not have personal logins, but must still authenticate by manually skipping the login process (hence the term *catch and release*).

The *Co-op Class* consists of users with prearranged login information. The rules for membership are usually determined by local community groups and configured in the central Auth system database. This class is typically granted much greater bandwidth and access to ports, as users can now be held accountable for their own actions.

The *Owner Class* is much the same as the Co-op Class, but is reserved for the owner of a given node and anyone else to whom they want to grant access. The Owner Class preempts traffic from all other classes and has free use of all network resources.

The typical connection process starts when a roaming user associates with the AP, and is immediately issued a DHCP lease, as shown in Figure 7-9. All access beyond contacting the Auth service is denied by default. When the user tries to browse the web, he is immediately redirected to the gateway service, which then redirects him to the Auth system's SSL login page (after appending a random token and some other information to the URL line).

The user is then presented with three choices: log in with his prearranged login information, click on a link to find out more about membership, or click the *Skip Login* button.

Once the user has either logged in correctly or skipped the process, the Auth system creates an outcome message, signs it with Pretty Good Privacy (PGP) encryption, and sends it back to the wireless gateway (see Figure 7-10).

The gateway has a copy of the Auth service's public PGP key and can verify the authenticity of the message. Part of the data included in the response is the random token that the gateway originally issued to the client, making it very difficult to fake out the gateway with a "replay attack." The digital

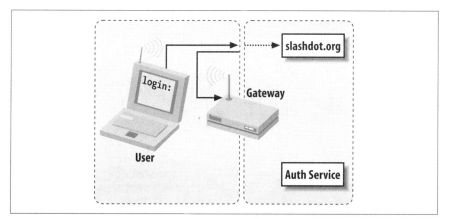

Figure 7-9. The user is immediately issued a lease, and his first web connection is redirected to the wireless gateway's service

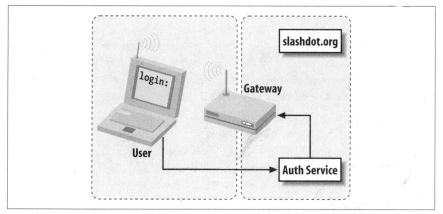

Figure 7-10. After login, the Auth system connects back to the wireless gateway and notifies it of the outcome; the gateway can then decide whether to grant further access

signature prevents the possibility of other machines posing as the Auth service and sending bogus messages to the wireless gateway.

Now, if all has gone well for the user, the wireless gateway modifies its firewall rules to grant further access, and redirects the user back to the site he wanted to browse (see Figure 7-11).

In order to keep the connection open, a small window is opened on the client side (via JavaScript) that refreshes the login page every few minutes. Once the user moves out of range or quits his browser, the connection is reset and requires another manual login.

The requirements on the gateway side are minimal (the system was designed to run under Linux 2.4 on a 486 with 16MB RAM). The Auth service is

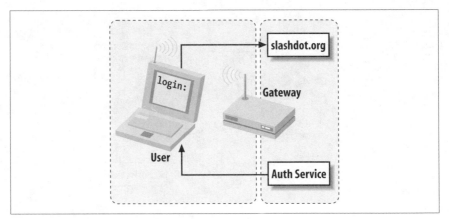

Figure 7-11. The user can now continue along his merry way

designed to be administered by a community group that maintains its user database in whatever way it sees fit. For example, running a node is one obvious way to become a co-op member. But that isn't always the best way to spend resources; people who contribute hardware, programming skill, bandwidth, or even meeting space and sandwiches should certainly be considered for membership. The technical aspects of catch and release are being solved, and it's up to everyone to work on the social details.

The NoCatAuth system is under active development, and now has a variety of new features. "Passive" mode allows operation without the connect-back phase (i.e., to work behind a NAT). There are also many additional back-end authentication methods, including PAM, RADIUS, TACACS+, and even IMAP. You can always get the latest version from *http://nocat.net*.

Fun with IP

Once your network project is in place, you may find that it will quickly grow beyond your expectations. What begins as a simple point-to-point link across the street might need to quickly expand to accommodate friends and neighbors, as they find out about "the network." As the network grows, the complexity of managing it grows as well. But then, this is the fun part. Here are some novel innovations that community groups are using to extend their projects into fun new areas. While they are not directly related to wireless networking, these ideas can enhance your wireless network.

Running Your Own Top-Level Domain in DNS

If you're using private address space for your wireless network and it grows to a respectable size, you will probably want to start offering local services (such as web servers and music streamers). But simply using IP addresses is no fun. Consider the ease of setting up your own top-level domain (TLD). Normally, zone entries in *named.conf* look something like this:

```
zone "oreillynet.com" {
        type master;
        file "data/oreillynet.com";
};
```

This is an entry appropriate for an authoritative DNS server for the *oreillynet.com* subdomain. The actual top-level domains (i.e., *.com*, *.net*, *.org*, *.int*, etc.) in use on the Internet are delegated only to the mysterious 13 known as the root DNS servers. Even though your DNS servers won't be consulted by the rest of the Internet, it can be handy to set up your very own TLD that works only on your wireless network.

For example, suppose your wireless network uses the private 10.42.5.0/24 network. These machines aren't reachable directly from the Internet, and you don't really want to advertise their DNS information to would-be network crackers. Try a non-standard TLD:

```
zone "cat" {
        type master;
        file "data/cat";
        allow-transfer { 10.42.5/24; };
        allow-query { 10.42.5/24; };
};
```

(We actually use *.cat* on the NoCat Network in Sebastopol. If you've ever wondered where the cat went, now you've found it.) With this added to your zone file, set up a master record for *.cat* just as you would any other domain:

```
$TTL 86400
@       IN SOA  ns.cat. root.homer.cat. (
                2002090100      ; Serial
                10800           ; Refresh after 3 hours
                3600            ; Retry after 1 hour
                604800          ; Expire (1 week)
                60              ; Negative expiry time
                )

        IN NS           ns.cat.

ns      IN A    10.42.5.1

homerIN A       10.42.5.10
bart IN A       10.42.5.11
lisa IN A       10.42.5.12
```

Reload the name server, and you should be able to simply ping *homer.cat*. If you'd like other name servers to maintain slave copies of your TLD, just add them as usual:

```
zone "cat" {
        type slave;
        file "db.cat";
        masters { 10.42.5.1; };
};
```

In this way, you can extend your new TLD across your entire private network architecture. Various network groups are using their own top-level and subdomain schemes as they come online. For example, SeattleWireless uses *.swn*, and I have *.rob.swn* delegated to my machine at home (10.15.6.1). How did I arrive at this number? And why would people in Sebastopol care about what I'm doing in Seattle? (Considering that a wireless link between the two is, well, quite improbable? Read on.)

Tunnels, Tunnels Everywhere

As we have discussed many times in this book, good wireless communication critically depends on having clean line of sight between two points. If there's an obstacle that you just can't go over, around, or through, then you simply can't have radio communications between those two points. Extremely long range (more than 40 miles or so) just can't be bridged in a single hop using the techniques and equipment described in this book. But suppose you are building out a community project that has a couple of pockets of wireless infrastructure that simply can't see each other. How can you build a large network that has a consistent address space if all of the points aren't directly connected by radio? If there is already an Internet connection at both points, then there is hope. One way to connect the unconnectable is to use the power of IP tunneling.

If you have never worked with IP tunneling, you might want to take a look at the Advanced Router HOWTO (*http://www.tldp.org/HOWTO/Adv-Routing-HOWTO/*) before continuing. Essentially, an IP tunnel is much like a VPN, except that not every IP tunnel involves encryption. A machine that is "tunneled" into another network has a virtual interface configured with an IP address that isn't local, but exists on a remote network. Usually, all (or most) network traffic is routed down this tunnel, so remote clients appear to exist on the network as if they were local. A tunnel can be used to allow clients from the Internet access to private network services, or more generally, to connect any two private networks by using the Internet to carry the tunnel traffic.

If you want to perform simple IP-within-IP tunneling between two machines, try IPIP. It is probably the simplest tunnel protocol available, and it works with *BSD, Solaris, and even Windows. Note that IPIP is simply a tunneling protocol, and does not involve any sort of encryption. Here is one method for establishing an IPIP tunnel in Linux.

Before we rush right into our first tunnel, you'll need a copy of the advanced routing tools (specifically the *ip* utility). You can get the latest authoritative copy from *ftp://ftp.inr.ac.ru/ip-routing/*. Be warned, the advanced routing tools aren't especially friendly, but they allow you to manipulate nearly any facet of the Linux networking engine.

In this example, I'll assume that you have two private networks (10.42.1.0/ 24 and 10.42.2.0/24) and that these networks both have direct Internet connectivity via a Linux router at each network. The "real" IP address of the first network router is 240.101.83.2, and the "real" IP address of the second router is 251.4.92.217. This isn't very difficult, so let's jump right in.

First, load the kernel module on both routers:

```
# modprobe ipip
```

Next, on the first network's router (on the 10.42.1.0/24 network), do the following:

```
# ip tunnel add mytun mode ipip remote 251.4.92.217 local 240.101.83.2
    ttl 255
# ifconfig mytun 10.42.1.1
# route add -net 10.42.2.0/24 dev tunl0
```

On the second network's router (on the 10.42.2.0/24), reciprocate:

```
# ip tunnel add mytun mode ipip remote 240.101.83.2 local 251.4.92.217
    ttl 255
# ifconfig tunl0 10.42.2.1
# route add -net 10.42.1.0/24 dev tunl0
```

Naturally, you can give the interface a more meaningful name than *mytun* if you like. From the first network's router, you should now be able to ping 10.42.2.1, and from the second network's router, you should be able to ping 10.42.1.1. Likewise, every machine on the 10.42.1.0/24 network should be able to route to every machine on the 10.42.2.0/24 network, as if the Internet weren't even there.

If you're running a Linux 2.2.x kernel, you're in luck: here's a shortcut that makes the advanced routing tools package unnecessary. After loading the module, try these commands:

```
# ifconfig tunl0 10.42.1.1 pointopoint 251.4.92.217
# route add -net 10.42.2.0/24 dev tunl0
```

And on the second network's router (10.42.2.0/24):

```
# ifconfig tunl0 10.42.2.1 pointopoint 240.101.83.2
# route add -net 10.42.1.0/24 dev tunl0
```

That's all there is to it.

If you can ping the opposite router, but other machines on the network don't seem to be able to pass traffic beyond the router, make sure that both routers are configured to forward packets between interfaces:

```
# echo "1" > /proc/sys/net/ipv4/ip_forward
```

If you need to reach networks beyond 10.42.1.0 and 10.42.2.0, simply add additional route add -net lines. There is no configuration needed on any of your network hosts, as long as they have a default route to their respective router (they definitely should; it *is* their router).

To close the tunnel, bring down the interface (and delete it, if you like) on both browsers:

```
# ifconfig mytun down
# ip tunnel del mytun
```

Or, in Linux 2.2:

```
# ifconfig tunl0 down
```

The kernel will very politely clean up your routing table for you when the interface goes away.

I am currently using IP tunneling to connect the NoCatNet project with SeattleWireless. Since we are organizing the use of the reserved 10 net space (see *http://freenetworks.org/* for the ad hoc IP allocation chart), we know that IP addresses won't be reused. To date, we have successfully made Voice-over-IP phone calls and shared web and streaming music data over multiple radio hops, through a couple of IP tunnels (spanning California to Washington), and again over several more radio hops. While radio links are always best (in terms of low latency, high bandwidth, and low cost), IP tunnels can help make the impossible a reality.

In Closing

802.11b networking is limited only by the imaginations of those who can get their hands on it—and with prices dropping as time goes on, the number of people who are hacking it will only increase. People are constantly pushing the boundaries of what is possible with wireless networking, community projects, and novel uses of the Internet. If you're interested in extending the gear, sign on to any of the great local wireless mailing lists, buy yourself some gear, and get started.

## CHAPTER 8

Radio Free Planet

The past few years have shown an explosion of interest in building wireless public networks. The ubiquity of affordable 802.11b gear has fueled enormous interest in extending the Net and providing open (or very low cost) access to it. The idea seems almost inevitable: if major wireless providers charge forty dollars or more *per month* for (comparatively) low-speed network access and tools are available to provide high-speed access yourself for very little cost, why not join in and make it happen? People all over the planet who have shared some part of the "unlimited free bandwidth everywhere" dream are building their own ubiquitous high-speed networks. By cooperating and using open standards, people are now building the infrastructure necessary to provide network access to thousands of simultaneous users, at very little cost to themselves. People everywhere are beginning to realize that this can be done more practically as a cooperative community service, rather than as a commercial venture with an ultimate cash profit motive.

When I started work on this book in early 2001, there were perhaps 10 well-known wireless groups in existence. When the first edition was published (in November of 2001), the wireless communities list at Personal Telco (*http://www.personaltelco.net/index.cgi/WirelessCommunities*) listed more that 50 projects. A year and a half later, that number has again increased fivefold, to more than 250 independent community wireless networking projects.

Here are a few of the biggest and most unique projects that I've come across. While by no means comprehensive, this introduction should give you an idea of what's going on (maybe even in your own neighborhood).

Seattle Wireless

Founders: **Matt Westervelt** and **Ken Caruso**
Location: **Seattle, Washington**
Project Started: **June 2000**
URL: *http://www.seattlewireless.net/*

Seattle Wireless has taken on one of the most ambitious projects of any community group: they intend to build a fully routed Metropolitan Area Network, independent of any commercial service provider. To this end, they are setting up their own top-level DNS domains, allocating private IP addresses, setting up backbone nodes, and managing the rollout of the network so that any wireless node will be able to reach any other without ever passing packets over a commercial network. As any backbone node is able to provide Internet gateway services, wireless clients can also access the Internet regardless of where they may physically be located in the city.

Because the entire wireless network doesn't ever rely on the wire, it keeps the operating cost of the network fixed, and gives it the capability to provide valuable communication services in the event of a major disaster (Seattle isn't exactly known for its stability, in many ways). Seattle has some unique geographical advantages that may help this approach: relatively few trees, many tall buildings, rolling hills, and a high concentration of technically capable alpha geeks. I'm sure the coffee doesn't hurt, either.

Their web site provides a terrific wealth of information, from network routing theory to antenna design. The Seattle Wireless web site was launched in September 2000. Since then, they have been mentioned or featured in dozens of publications, ranging from *Wired* magazine to *Le Monde,* a major newspaper in France. They also have a huge mailing list following and hold regular meetings. They are making things happen in the Great Northwest.

Bay Area Wireless Users Group (BAWUG)

Founders: **Matt Peterson, Cliff Skolnick**, and **Tim Pozar**
Location: **San Francisco Bay area**
Project started: **September 2000**
URL: *http://www.bawug.org/*

With the understanding that wireless access can significantly reduce the cost of Internet access while making it easier to share resources, BWUG was founded to promote wireless use for the greater San Francisco Bay area. They hold bimonthly meetings to pool knowledge and educate people about a variety of wireless topics. While their motto is "we don't build networks," they do attract a large number of participants. The BAWUG mailing list currently has nearly 2000 subscribers, and meetings draw an average of 40 people.

The BAWUG attracts a wide range of interested parties, from VCs and start-ups to HAMs, sysadmins, activists, and the general public. Many groups that do build networks have spun off from BAWUG, including sfwireless.net, sflan.com, and bawrn.org. BAWUG itself also worked with FreeNet-works.org to build the network at the 2002 ApacheCon.

The BAWUG grew out of PlayaNet, the free 802.11b network of Burning Man (see *http://www.playanet.org/* and *http://www.burningman.com/* for details). Since a huge percentage of Burning Man attendees are from San Francisco, it was only natural that the 10-day-a-year PlayaNet geeks would want something to work on for the other 355.

If you're ever in the SF Bay area, I highly recommend attending a meeting. They have often hosted an interesting collection of speakers, ranging from wireless industry jockeys to Internet startups to hardcore RF hacks. It has been well worth the two-hour drive from Sebastopol each time our group has attended.

PersonalTelco

Founder: **Adam Shand**
Location: **Portland, Oregon**
Project started: **November 2000**
URL: *http://www.personaltelco.net/*

PersonalTelco's mission statement is: "To promote and build public wire-less networks through community support and education."

PersonalTelco has been very active in the Portland area since the end of 2000. Their members provide about 80 hot spots throughout the Portland area, and their mailing lists reach about 700 interested people. Personal-Telco's regular monthly meetings draw about 50 people on average.

The PersonalTelco Project is incorporated as a 501(c)3 nonprofit, allowing them to accept tax-deductible donations to put toward projects for the pub-lic good. They also host the definitive community networking project list (with over 250+ projects listed at the time of this writing) at *http://www.personaltelco.net/index.cgi/WirelessCommunities*.

In June of 2001, PersonalTelco hosted the first ever Wireless Community Networking summit. Organizers from Seattle, New York, British Columbia, Portland, San Francisco Bay, and Sebastopol were there. We had a very pro-ductive couple of days, covering divergent topics such as antenna design, network layout, the FCC, and "catch and release" captive portals. There was a tremendous energy and goodwill between the groups, as we all realized we were in this experiment together.

NYCwireless

Founders: **Terry Schmidt, Anthony Townsend, Ben Serebin, Jacob Farkas,** and **Dustin Goodwin**
Location: **New York City**
Project started: **May 2001**
URL: *http://nycwireless.net/*

NYCwireless has four major goals:

1. Provide public hotspots, especially at parks and independent coffee shops
2. Advocate the use of wireless technology, particularly consumer-owned, unlicensed, low-cost equipment
3. Educate the public about wireless technology issues, including installation, tinkering, security, and applications
4. Provide emergency communications that don't depend on existing infrastructure

In order to better serve their first goal (providing hotspots), NYCwireless contracts with a for-profit company (Cloud Networks, Inc.), which is staffed by some of NYCwireless's founding members. This helps to allow NYCwireless itself to focus on education and advocacy, and not get bogged down in projects that its volunteer members cannot devote time and resources to complete. Cloud Networks gives deep discounts for NYCwireless projects (anywhere from 50–100% depending on available external funding), which helps keep projects both active and well-supplied.

NYCwireless has over 100 active nodes throughout New York City. The Bryant Park Wireless Network is their flagship node; it averaged in excess of 50 users per day during the summer of 2002. They expect that number to double next summer. They also helped provide emergency communications in the days following 9/11/01, quickly assembling free access nodes in areas that had no other telecommunication facilities available.

Their main strategy has been to partner with local government and quasi-governmental neighborhood associations to help bring about their goals. Local government sees value in community-based wireless and helps provide the resources that make many NYCwireless projects possible.

Houston Wireless

Founders: **Steven Byrnes, Barrett Canon,** and **Matthew Solnik**
Location: **Houston, Texas**
Project started: **Summer 2001**
URL: *http://www.houstonwireless.org/*

Also known as the Houston Wireless Users Group, Houston Wireless supports the following primary goals:

1. Promote pervasive, high-speed wireless access in urban and suburban areas. While the telcos are slowly rolling out new technologies, third-generation wireless (3G) is realistically still years away. Houston Wireless uses affordable technology that is here now, which makes it easier for the average person to get involved in wireless networking.

2. Research and experiment with networking protocols using wireless (e.g., IPsec, Mobile IP, and IPv6).

3. Experiment with new wireless technologies (e.g., 802.11a, 802.11g, and UWB).

4. To have fun. :-)

Houston Wireless has about 30 nodes online and over 100 people on their various mailing lists. They sponsor active monthly meetings (averaging about 25 people at the time of this writing).

Universal Wireless

The community wireless networking bug isn't constrained to the U.S. Networking projects in dozens of countries are now online, with more joining in every day. Here are just a few of the international efforts underway:

BC Wireless

Founder: **Matthew Asham**
Location: **British Columbia, Canada**
Project started: **December 2000**
URL: *http://bcwireless.net/*

BC Wireless focuses on showing consumers how to use license-exempt technology to connect themselves with other people. This ranges from answering simple questions about 802.11b to talking about wide-scale infrastructural networking. Much like BAWUG, the BC Wireless project itself isn't really a networking project. BC Wireless is more of a resource used by its members as a reference tool. Many members of BC Wireless work on projects independently of each other.

BC Wireless's particular focus is to bridge the digital divide that separates network hackers from the average person. They want to help people learn to effectively use technology for themselves and to embrace it, rather than to be afraid of it. They are working with the local public school system to help children learn networking skills, particularly in impoverished communities where money and education are scarce.

They are also actively working on documentation and software for average users, to help assist people in setting up their own web sites and home networks.

Consume

Founders: **Simon Anderson, Ben Laurie, Adam Laurie, Julian Priest,** and **James Stevens**
Location: **London, England**
Project started: **August 2000**
URL: *http://www.consume.net/*

Consume the Net! Consume is "a collaborative strategy for the self provision of a broadband telecommunications infrastructure." They are building a free network in England, and to that end they host extensive FAQs, provide mailing lists, and even have their own online node database. Much like the SeattleWireless effort, Consume is building a wireless infrastructure independent of the local monopoly-held wired network.

Melbourne Wireless

Founders: **Steven Haigh, Glen Brunning,** and **Drew Ulricksen**
Location: **Melbourne, Victoria, Australia**
Project started: **June 2000**
URL: *http://melbourne.wireless.org.au*

Melbourne Wireless, Inc. is a not-for-profit group aiming to establish a fast, free, metropolitan area wireless network based on existing off-the-shelf 802.11-based equipment.

Melbourne Wireless lists over 1,200 nodes under way in their LocFinder database, of which 225 are active as of this writing. They hold regular monthly meetings and host the usual assortment of online resources (including FAQs, news, and mailing lists).

RedLibre

Founder: **Jaime Robles**
Location: **Madrid, Spain**
Project started: **September 2001**
URL: *http://www.redlibre.net/*

RedLibre was the first wireless group in Spain. They are an organizational group that helps coordinate people and resources with various local community wireless groups throughout Spain. RedLibre had a national meeting in December, 2002 and met with representatives from 15 local wireless groups. Through their coordination, Spain has an exceptionally well-developed wireless community presence.

The RedLibre network has active free wireless nodes in five cities throughout Spain. They have over 1,100 registered users and more than 500 people subscribe to their mailing lists.

Wireless Leiden

Founders: **Jasper Koolhaas, Marten Vijn, Evert Verduin, Johan de Stigter,** and **Rudi van Drunen**
Location: **Leiden, Netherlands**
Project started: **September 2001**
URL: *http://www.wirelessleiden.nl/*

The town of Leiden (in the West Netherlands) has had a particularly successful community network project, involving local government, businesses, and private individuals. From their web site:

> In this group of enthusiastic and knowledgeable professional volunteers who wanted to experiment with wireless connections, the ambition of developing a non-commercial, fast and open (for everyone, also commercial enterprises) network has emerged. Anyone cooperating with the group will be having access to an extremely fast network, even capable of sharing high-quality audio, video or TV images. In the starting phase the group was working on the technology trying to answer the question: **"can it be done?"** Now the answer is **"Yes,"** proof-of-concept has been delivered.

What started as a hobbyist project in September of 2001 has evolved into a nonprofit foundation with over 300 active users. Wireless Leiden is a terrific example of how commercial enterprises can benefit from free networks. Employees frequently use the public infrastructure to telecommute to work, using encrypted tunnels to keep their traffic secure. Through cooperation with local schools, churches, and businesses, Wireless Leiden has built one of the most advanced free networks on the planet.

The Future

With support from all over the globe, community wireless projects are bringing people together to build a communications network focused on utility, not profit. This project has brought more geeks out from behind their computer screens than any other I've encountered. These people are moved to get out, meet their neighbors, and build something new out of a simple desire to communicate with each other. From every indication, the community wireless network seems to be an idea whose time has finally come.

## CHAPTER 9

Radio Free Sebastopol

My first brush with 802.11b networking in the summer of 2000 demonstrated something very clear to me, even then: it was obvious that wireless connectivity was going to be a tremendously important technology. In the next few years, hundreds of local community wireless groups and commercial ventures have sprung up, building usable networks over the air using 802.11 technology. This is the story of how an idea to make our corporate network more flexible has evolved, and has become part of a worldwide movement to provide ubiquitous wireless network access.

OSCON 2000

My initial introduction to wireless networking was in Monterey, California, at OSCON (Open Source Conference) 2000. O'Reilly arranged free public wireless access for conference attendees. The tremendous flexibility of being able to connect to the network from anywhere led to all sorts of interesting, unforeseen interactions. For example, people attending a large talk could converse in real time over IRC and discuss the talk (and even critique the speaker) without raising their voices. They could use the Net as a resource when asking the speaker questions, to draw out very interesting points by way of real-time examples. With an instant messaging client, ubiquitous wireless made an effective, free, two-way paging system. (Rather than trying to use the overloaded PCS phone system, it was now possible to send a quick "Where do you want to meet for lunch?" message, and get a response back instantly.) Conference attendees no longer had to return to their hotel rooms for dialup access, or be banished to a terminal room away from where the action was, just to check their email or refer to a web page. That was assuming, of course, that one had an 802.11b card and laptop handy. Personally, I had to wrestle a card away from a buddy who happened to have a spare. I realized that networking on borrowed time wouldn't cut it; I simply had to pack my own.

On returning from OSCON, there was much interest at O'Reilly in getting wireless networking going at the office. If that much flexibility could be put in place for very low cost, why weren't we using it in-house? If conference-goers could use the stuff to grill speakers for information more effectively, what could it do for our company meetings and presentations? And so, without even knowing my Direct Sequence from my Spread Spectrum, I started down the long, winding path of wireless networking.

The Campus

After setting up a couple of access points to cover our campus, and a crash course in WEP, MAC filtering, and closed networks, our fledgling 802.11b network was up. With relatively little effort and expense (about $3000 and a few hours work in all), we now had seamless coverage in all three of our buildings, complete with roaming between APs. At the time, the main O'Reilly offices in Sebastopol consisted of three two-story buildings, covering an area about 450 by 150 feet. Using one Lucent AP-1000 in each building, and a small 5db omni at each AP, I was able to cover nearly all of the offices and conference rooms.

Early on in the process, one of our users noticed that she couldn't get online, even though she had a very strong signal. Upon checking her network settings, I realized that she hadn't set her ESSID, and was therefore associating with any available network. It just so happened that the network with the strongest signal was coming from the business next door! I fired up Lucent's Site Map tool, and, sure enough, there was an existing 802.11b network immediately next door. After a quick conversation with their sysadmin, we decided on a channel numbering scheme that would minimize interference between the two networks. (This is exactly why a preliminary site survey is so important: even though you may not see antennas, a network may already exist in your area! Don't just assume that since wireless is new to you, it's new to your part of town.)

Now that our offices were saturated with access, with 50+ users up and happily untethered, what could we do with it next? Naturally, more than a few eyes turned to the hotel and coffee shop across the street. If one could get a signal from the hotel, then visiting employees who stayed there could get online for free, at 11Mbps (as opposed to paying per minute for a trickle of dialup access). And of course, being able to work directly from the coffee shop must do *something* for productivity. With visions of mochas and bandwidth dancing in my head, I looked into adding external antennas to increase our range.

Coffee, Coffee, Coffee

In about a week, I had an omnidirectional antenna installed on the roof, and 25 feet of LMR-200 running down to our access point. Why did I use 25 feet of cable that loses almost 17db of signal every hundred feet? And why did I use an omni, when a tight sector or patch antenna would have made more sense? Because in early 2000, without any prior background in radio, I went with what our vendor had to offer: a 25 foot run of so-called "low-loss" microwave antenna cable, and an expensive omnidirectional popsicle stick (after all, if Lucent made the gear, it *must* be compatible with a Lucent access point, right?).

Luckily for me, even with the high line loss, the omni managed to do the job. That afternoon, I walked across the street, ordered an iced mocha, and merrily typed out the confirmation email. As I hit *Ctrl-X Y*, I was compelled to meditate on that inevitable question, "What next?" If it was possible to get a good signal about 1,500 feet from the AP, how feasible would it be to provide wireless access to our local employees? After all, many of our people live in the area and were using dialup to access our network from home. Would it be possible to provide a fast wireless connection to anyone who was within range? Just how far could this technology be stretched?

Online From Home, No Strings Attached

Around this time, I relocated to Sebastopol from San Francisco. By a staggering coincidence, the house we moved into happened to have clean line of sight to the antenna I had installed on the roof, more than half of a mile away. This provided a great tool for experimentation, as I now had a fixed signal at a distance with clear LOS, and could aim whatever kind of equipment I liked at it to see how well it would perform. I realized that a high-gain dish, pointed directly at the omni, could achieve a very good signal, even through walls and glass. I was so excited by the quality of the signal that I bungee-corded the dish to a chair with rollers, and rolled it around the house, while streaming a full-screen video on my laptop the entire time. Yes, a keen interest in wireless was now developing into a full-blown psychotic obsession, as the potential possibilities of long-distance, low-cost, high-speed communications played about in my mind.

I finally mounted the dish inside my attic, set up a makeshift access point, and found that I could have a stable 11Mbps connection from about six-tenths of a mile away, with a "stealth" dish under my roof that wouldn't bother the neighbors. I used this connection for several months, through all kinds of weather (and I was very grateful of it: in my area, DSL and cable modems weren't an option at the time).

Now that I had a proof-of-concept and parts list, I approached others in the company who live in the area, to try to set up a second node. This was when I came up against possibly the biggest natural obstacle to long-distance microwave: *trees*. As it turned out, I had been truly lucky with my own situation. Finding many clean paths to a single point is highly improbable in Sebastopol. Except for the immediate downtown area, medium to dense foliage is virtually everywhere. After visiting several possible node sites (and trying to shoot to O'Reilly despite the trees), it became clear that a single access point at a low altitude wasn't going to be sufficient to get our Sebastopol employees unplugged. There are just too many trees between O'Reilly and the rest of the world.

With no obvious plan of action, I had to put the wireless extension project away for a while, so I could do more research. By now, there was certainly no shortage of online information available, as community groups began popping up all over the globe. I decided that if I was going to get anywhere with practical wireless networking, I'd need to talk to some experts.

Seattle Wireless

The following March, I took a trip to Seattle. My brother was moving to the area, so I took the opportunity to travel with him up north to see the Seattle Wireless network for myself. I must admit that I wasn't fully prepared (psychologically) for what I found when I got there. Here were a bunch of *very* sharp sysadmins, programmers, and net monkeys, who were gearing up to build a redundant, fully routed public network, independent of the Internet. They were working on this project *entirely in their spare time*, with no promise of reward other than the joy of hacking out a project that simply needed to be done. They weren't just hooking up a couple of APs and trusting their luck; they had an entire network topology planned, a hardware solution down, and nodes in the works to connect sites miles apart.

I spent a day building antennas and speculating about the possibilities of 802.11b with the SWN crowd. By the end of the day, we managed to put together a yagi made out of washers, some tubing, a bolt, and a pie tin that carried an 11Mbps signal about a mile. The topography of Seattle is such that their network plans will probably work: tall buildings, rolling hills, and limited tree cover makes much of the city accessible (assuming one can get on top of the hills). I went back to Sebastopol with a couple of important realizations:

- There was tremendous interest in high-speed wireless networking, even among people who already had high-speed wired access. Ubiquitous wireless seemed to be almost as much in demand as DSL and cable modems.

- The seemingly insurmountable difficulty of finding LOS between points can't really be approached by one person or group. But a larger community, working together toward the same goal, can bring a lot of resources to bear on any problem.

- Wireless networking isn't as simple as replacing a piece of CAT5 with a radio. Radio has many strange properties that are completely alien to people who have been studying computers and networking for years.

- Conversely, many radio experts find themselves lost when dealing with the intricacies of Internet networking (until very recently, a 9600 baud packet radio connection to a computer running a DOS TCP/IP stack was considered high tech in many circles). If we intend to push 802.11b beyond its intended limits, the plateau of knowledge that separates hardcore network jockeys from hardcore radio geeks *must* be crossed.

Ironically, it started to look like it would be easier to get the entire Sebastopol area unplugged with open network access, rather than try to connect a few users to a private network. But to do that, I certainly couldn't do all of the work. I needed to find out if there was as much interest in my area as there seemed to be in the rest of the country.

NoCat

It was obvious that we needed a local repository for information about forming a cooperative community network. Within a couple of days, some friends and I put together a simple web site and mailing list. But what to call it?

While sitting on the couch in the living room, logging in to check on something at work, my login fortune struck me as particularly funny, so I read it aloud to my friend Cat:

> You see, wire telegraph is a kind of a very, very long cat. You pull his tail in New York and his head is meowing in Los Angeles. Do you understand this? And radio operates exactly the same way: you send signals here, they receive them there. The only difference is that there is *no cat*. –Albert Einstein

Cat quickly replied, "That's what you should call this thing: No Cat." I immediately checked *whois* and saw that *nocat.net* was free. That settled it.

NoCat became the central repository for several wireless projects that Schuyler Erle (Perl programmer extraordinaire and wireless sympathizer from O'Reilly), myself, and others had been working on. We put together WRP, a wireless router-on-a-floppy to make setting up a wireless gateway quick and painless. We also started work on the NoCatAuth project, a method for authenticating users to a cooperative network without using any of the built-in (and limited) authentication methods available in the 802.11b specification. We also set up a mailing list for locals interested in wireless. Now that we had a web presence and some information available, we needed a way to connect with people in the local community.

The Community Takes Notice

Luckily, we didn't have to wait very long for the community to notice us. Just after I returned from Seattle, a local newspaper (*The Press Democrat*, *http://www.pressdemo.com/business/columns/02sims.html*) ran a feature on some of my wireless shenanigans. I had no idea at the time how valuable this kind of exposure could be to the community LAN idea. Within a week, I had received a few dozen emails and several phone calls from locals who were interested in wireless networking. Some offered expertise and equipment, while others were simply curious about our plans and what could be accomplished with 802.11b.

After the article ran, our mailing list grew to about 25 people. We decided to hold a general meeting to get organized and figure out what we wanted to do with this stuff. I was pleasantly surprised when 16 interested people showed up at that first meeting. Many were looking for free high-speed access, while others were simply curious. A few were Northpoint victims who had been forcibly unplugged from their DSL when that company went under, and they were looking for any alternative (apparently, they were no longer considered part of the "prime" market, and would likely not see high-speed access again for quite a while).

As the discussion went well into the third hour, it was obvious from that first meeting that this was going to turn into a regular event. These people were keenly interested in contributing to a free local network, and had a tremendous amount of knowledge and resources among them. But until now, they had no good way of connecting with each other. From this first get-together, all sorts of possibilities began to present themselves.

The general consensus was that, if people who had high-speed Net access wanted to share with those who wanted it but, for whatever reason, could not get it, there were several technical obstacles that needed to be overcome:

- The solution couldn't cost thousands of dollars, or else no one could afford it.
- There had to be a secure and easy way of figuring out who was who, and limiting what they could do on the network (so that node owners wouldn't be exposed to abusers, or have their hard-earned bandwidth monopolized by a freeloading few).
- The solution needed to be easy for someone with limited skills to set up, and require little or no maintenance.
- There had to be an easy way for people interested in point-to-point links to meet with each other.
- People who did have a fair idea of how to proceed needed access to all sorts of information, from choosing microwave connectors to configuring laptops.

We had some answers to these issues, but it became clear that these were going to be long-term problems, shared by anyone attempting to put together a community group. We put as much information as we could up at NoCat and pointed to others who had answers whenever possible.

The nearest wireless community group to Sebastopol was the BAWUG, who met regularly in the San Jose area. Since we were obviously working on parallel lines, it seemed to be time to see what our neighbors to the south were up to. I got a couple of local wireless zealots together and we made the two-hour trek to San Jose for a meeting.

The June 2001 BAWUG meeting was a great opportunity to network further. Much like our Sebastopol meeting, there were people with all different abilities and expectations present (only here there were about 50 of them!). After a couple of interesting presentations, I got a chance to talk with antenna gurus, some Apple Airport hackers, and even a commercial wireless startup.

There was much buzz about the impending Portland Summit meeting: wireless community leaders from all over were going to converge on Portland for a weekend of planning, talk, beer, and general hackery. This was a meeting I could not miss.

The Portland Summit

That June, for the first time ever, people from community wireless networks across the country (and even from Canada!) met in Portland to talk about what we were up to. Organizers from Seattle, New York, British Columbia, Portland, the San Francisco Bay area, and Sebastopol were there. We had a very productive couple of days, covering divergent topics such as antenna design, network layout, the FCC, and "catch and release" captive portals. There was a tremendous energy and goodwill between the groups, as we all realized we were in this experiment together (admittedly, the beer probably helped a bit, too).

I think Portland was very reassuring for all of us, because it brought together people from all over the globe who shared a common vision: unlimited free bandwidth everywhere. We had developed these ideas independently, and while some of the details of how we were attempting this feat diverged, the ultimate intent was the same. The era of wireless community network access had arrived: hardware, software, and network backbone were all becoming cheap and ubiquitous enough to make it happen. All of our groups wanted to strengthen our local communities by bringing network access to anyone who cared to be a part of it. And by working together, sharing what we'd learned, giving away software, and pooling our collective efforts, we found that we could reach this goal faster than by trying to work out a solution on our own.

And So On

As I write this, we have just finished our third international "Community Wireless Summit," which brought almost 200 people to Santa Clara (the second happened in Seattle and had nearly the same attendance). NoCat now hosts two mailing lists that reach nearly 1,000 people. The NoCat network (*http://nocat.net/*) has grown to more than 20 active nodes (including two 11.5 mile hops), extending the reach of broadband access well beyond the "DSL divide."

With cooperative effort and wireless technology, the Internet is rapidly becoming more and more pervasive. My direct experience with people working on this project has turned up an important common thread: free access to information is in constant demand, and barriers to that access cause pain. I believe that working to provide free and unrestricted access to local networks (and ultimately, the Internet) is a benefit not only to one's local community, but to the world at large. I hope that this book has helped you to realize your goals and has helped you become more connected to your local community.

Regulations Affecting 802.11 Deployment

This is Tim Pozar's paper on the implications of FCC regulations regarding 802.11 networks. The original is available online at *http://www.lns.com/papers/part15/*.

Disclaimer

I am not a lawyer. Do not use my presentation as an authoritative guide on how to run your life, hobby, or business. The following is my interpretation of some the laws and regulations pertaining to 802.11 networks. Although this document has been reviewed by a number of telecommunications lawyers and experts in the field,* my advice may not hold up in the eyes of the the Federal Communications Commission (FCC) or in a court of law. This paper's purpose is to alert you to 802.11 deployment issues and offer some possible solutions to common regulatory problems. You may want to bring up these issues with your attorney, or research them yourself to see how they might affect you.

I am a long-time broadcast engineer and a member of the Society of Broadcast Engineers. I am also an active member of the Bay Area Wireless Users Group (BAWUG), so I have my foot in both the "conservative old-timer" and "excited newcomer" camps. With BAWUG, I promote the use of unlicensed spectrum to create and bridge communities. At the same time, I encourage what the FCC calls "good engineering practice" in the deployment of these networks.

---

* Many thanks to Mike Newman, Dewayne Hendricks, Dane Ericksen, Jim Thompson, Phil Kane, and others who reviewed this document!

As regulations change, you may want to refer to my web site (*http://www.lns. com*) for updates to this paper. Also, please send any comments, additions, or corrections concerning this paper to *pozar@lns.com*. Thanks in advance.

Abstract and Objectives

Many companies are jumping onto the wireless bandwagon by creating new "first mile" infrastructure in order to link to customers who do not yet have high-speed Internet access. They may also create this infrastructure to bypass the current wired solutions—it is often cheaper and easier to provide high-speed data to customers via a wireless link.

These are good ideas, but many Internet companies have little or no clue about the ramifications of using unlicensed spectrum. My purpose in writing this paper is to shed a little light on the law, policy, rules, regulations, and future developments that will affect wireless deployment.

1   Introduction to the Technology

802.11 is a standards group under the IEEE that develops standards related to wireless and wired Ethernet transmission. This includes the actual physical layer, including 802.11a and 802.11b modulation schemes.

802.11b is a Direct Sequence Spread Spectrum technology that, in the United States, occupies 11 channels centered on frequencies in the Industrial, Scientific, and Medical (ISM) band from 2.412 to 2.462GHz, in 5MHz steps. The spectrum used by a single 802.11b signal is 22MHz wide. Because the channels are smaller than the occupied bandwidth, only three channels (1, 6, and 11) can be used in a small area without running into interference.

802.11a doesn't use Direct Sequence. Instead it uses a modulation scheme called Orthogonal Frequency Division Multiplexing (OFDM). OFDM uses 52 300KHz-wide carriers grouped into one 20MHz-wide channel. The slower symbol speed of OFDM and the forward error correction incorporated into 802.11a make it more resilient to multi-path and interference. However, because 802.11a is broadcast at more than double the frequency of 802.11b, there is greater free space loss. An 802.11a installation with gain antennas and powered transmitters has a signal strength that is about 18 percent weaker than that of a similar 802.11b setup.

While 802.11b occupies the portion of the ISM band at 2.4GHz, 802.11a can occupy either the ISM band at 5.8GHz (5.725 to 5.850GHz), or a section of spectrum known as the Unlicensed National Information Infrastructure (U-NII) band. This band was approved in 1997 and promoted by the group WINForum, which was made up of individuals and companies such as Apple Computer.

The band takes up 300MHz of spectrum and is divided into three 100MHz sections. The first two are next to each other, and the third is 375MHz up from the top of the second band. The "low" band runs from 5.15GHz to 5.25GHz, the "middle" band runs from 5.25GHz to 5.35GHz, and the "high" band runs from 5.725 GHz to 5.825 GHz.* †

2   Regulations and Laws Affecting 802.11 Network Deployment

2.1   The Civilian Spectrum Regulations

The spectrum is managed by a number of different organizations. The most visible to the general public is the Federal Communications Commission (FCC). The FCC manages civilian, state, and local government usage of the radio spectrum. This is the regulatory organization that affects you.

The FCC has a set of rules and regulations that define use of spectrum, as well as policies and procedures for working with the FCC. You can obtain these in hardcopy by ordering the *Code of Federal Regulations, Title 47* from the Government Printing Office (GPO) at *http://bookstore.gpo.gov/*.

Companies such as Pike and Fischer (*http://www.pf.com/*) offer subscription services to the updated FCC regulations, policies, and proposed rules. There are also free (but slightly dated) versions of the FCC rules online. The "Hypertext FCC Rules Project" run by Harold Hallikainen at *http://www. hallikainen.com/FccRules* is one such project.

Harold's site actually indexes the GPO's online version of the rules. You can go directly to the GPO's online version of the rules at *http://www.access.gpo. gov/nara/cfr/cfr-table-search.html*.

The GPO's site points to all of the Code of Federal Regulations (CFR); you want the section labeled *Title 47 - Telecommunication*.

---

* The FCC currently has a Notice of Proposed Rulemaking, or NPRM (RM-10371), to add 5.470 to 5.725GHz to the U-NII band.

† Note that the ISM band actually goes another 25MHz higher than the "high" portion of the U-NII band.

2.2   Enforcement

The FCC has the authority to investigate any user of the band. In fact, they can actually come onsite and inspect the operation of equipment:

> 15.29(a) Any equipment or device subject to the provisions of this part, together with any certificate, notice of registration or any technical data required to be kept on file by the operator, supplier or party responsible for compliance of the device shall be made available for inspection by a Commission representative upon reasonable request.

The FCC has very limited resources for enforcement—the trend for the last couple of decades has been toward deregulation and the reduction of staffing in the enforcement bureaus. The FCC will usually not visit you unless they receive a complaint. There have been rare reports of the FCC going after WISPs when they interfered with Part 97 (amateur radio) users. Working with the co-users of these bands is in your best interest, as they will be the ones complaining.

The National Telecommunications and Information Administration (NTIA) works with the Interdepartmental Radio Advisory Committee (IRAC), which manages federal use of the spectrum. You are not likely to hear from them unless you've done something really wrong.

3   Power Limits

Ideally, a well-engineered path has just the amount of power required to get from point A to point B with decent reliability. Good engineering limits the signal to the area being served, which results in reduced interference and a more efficient use of the spectrum. Using too much power will cover more area than is needed and may interfere with other users of the band.

Because 802.11 is designed for short-range use in offices and homes, it is limited to very low power.

3.1   FCC 15.247 and 80211.b

Section 15.247 of the FCC regulations covers the operation of 802.11b devices.

3.1.1   Point-to-multipoint communication

You are allowed up to 30dBm or 1 watt of Transmitter Power Output (TPO) with a 6dBi antenna, or 36dBm or 4 watts Effective Isotropic Radiated Power (EIRP). The TPO must be reduced 1dB for every dB of antenna gain over 6dBi.

3.1.2   Point-to-point communication

The FCC encourages directional antennas to minimize interference with other users. The FCC is more lenient with point-to-point links: the TPO must be reduced by one-third of a dB, instead of the full dB for point-to-multipoint communication.

More specifically, for every 3dB of antenna gain over a 6dBi antenna, you must reduce the TPO 1dB below one watt. For example, a 24dBi antenna is 18dB over a 6dBi antenna. You would have to lower a one-watt (30dBm) transmitter 6dB (one-third of 18) to 24dBm or one-quarter watt.

3.2   FCC 15.407 and 802.11a

Section 15.407 of the FCC regulations covers the operation of 802.11a devices.

3.2.1   Point-to-multipoint communication

As described previously, the U-NII band is chopped into three sections. The "low" band runs from 5.15GHz to 5.25GHz and has a maximum power of 50mW (TPO). This band is meant for in-building use only, as defined by sections 15.407 (d) and (e):

> (d) Any U-NII device that operates in the 5.15–5.25 GHz band shall use a transmitting antenna that is an integral part of the device.
>
> (e) Within the 5.15–5.25 GHz band, U-NII devices will be restricted to indoor operations to reduce any potential for harmful interference to co-channel MSS operations.

The "middle" band runs from 5.25GHz to 5.35GHz, with a maximum power limit of 250mW. Finally, the "high" band runs from 5.725GHz to 5.825GHz, and has a maximum transmitter power of 1 watt and an antenna gain of 6dBi/36dBm/4 watts EIRP.

3.2.2   Point-to-point communication

As with 802.11b, the FCC does give some latitude to point-to-point links in 15.407(a)(3). For the 5.725GHz to 5.825GHz band, the FCC allows a TPO of 1 watt and up to a 23dBi gain antenna without requiring reduction of the TPO 1dB for every 1dB of gain over 23dBi.

15.247(b)(3)(ii) does allow the use of any gain antenna for point-to-point operations without reduction of the TPO for the 5.725GHz to 5.825GHz band. Look at the Part your equipment is certified under to see which EIRP restrictions apply.

4   Equipment Limitations and Certification

4.1   Certification

Part 15 devices are designed to be installed and used by the general public. With this in mind, the commission wants them to be as "idiot-proof" as possible. They have severe limitations on what you can do with this gear. For instance, the rules state that:

> 15.203 - An intentional radiator shall be designed to ensure that no antenna other than that furnished by the responsible party shall be used with the device.

A bit further in, the same sentiment is repeated:

> 15.204(c) - Only the antenna with which an intentional radiator is authorized may be used with the intentional radiator.

The basics of certification can be found in FCC 2.901 through 2.1093. The requirement for Part 15 devices can be found in 15.201.

Equipment can be certified in two ways: as a *component* or *system*. Component certification applies to equipment such as transmitters, amplifiers, or antennas. All can be mixed and matched with each other. However, if you have various equipment certified as a system, the parts of that system can't be used with other equipment. See 15.203 and 15.204:

> 15.204(b) - A transmission system consisting of an intentional radiator, an external radio frequency power amplifier, and an antenna, may be authorized, marketed and used under this part. **However, when a transmission system is authorized as a system, it must always be marketed as a complete system and must always be used in the configuration in which it was authorized. An external radio frequency power amplifier shall be marketed only in the system configuration with which the amplifier is authorized and shall not be marketed as a separate product.** [Boldface added by author for emphasis]

In other words, you can't take an AP that is certified as a system and attach an antenna that isn't a part of its certification.

You can, however, recertify equipment. If you go out and purchase gear on the street, there isn't anything to stop you from reselling this gear and recertifying it at the time of sale. There seems to be some discussion as to whether you need approval from the manufacturer for recertification, but I talked to one communications law attorney who said that approval is not needed.

Certification is an involved process and can be costly. You should contract with many of the consultants in this field for guidance.

4.2   Temporary Options to Certification

4.2.1   Experimental licenses: Part 5
Special Temporary Authorities (STAs): Parts 15.7 and 5.61

Experimental licenses are used for temporary experimentation, while STAs are issued for spectrum use in emergencies or other critical situations. In cases where time constraints make it impossible to go through the traditional paperwork process imposed by the FCC, an STA is granted. STAs are limited to six months of authorization, while experimental licenses can last for up to two years. STAs have a lower priority for interference than experimental licenses, but since they are issued to Part 15 devices, this doesn't matter much.

STAs and experimental licenses can be used only for very specific purposes, such as legitimate educational research. For instance, they cannot be used to "determine customer acceptance of a product" or for "marketing strategy."

For more information, visit the FCC web pages on STAs and experimental licenses at *http://www.fcc.gov/oet/info/filing/elb/*.

5   Interference

> This device complies with part 15 of the FCC Rules. Operation is subject to the following two conditions: (1) This device may not cause **harmful interference**, and (2) this device must accept any interference received, including interference that may cause undesired operation.
>
> [Labeling requirement in Part 15.19]

5.1   Description

Of course, interference is typically the state of the signal you are interested in while it's being destructively overpowered by a signal you are not interested in.

The FCC has a specific definition of "harmful interference":

> Part 2.1(c) **Harmful interference** - Interference which endangers the functioning of a radio-navigation service or of other safety services or seriously degrades, obstructs, or repeatedly interrupts a radio-communication service operating in accordance with these [International Radio] Regulations.

In Part 15 it is repeated as:

> Part 15.3(m) **Harmful interference**.
>
> Any emission, radiation or induction that endangers the functioning of a radio navigation service or of other safety services or seriously degrades,

obstructs or repeatedly interrupts a radio communications service operating in accordance with this chapter.

Interference will be a factor in your deployment. The 2.4GHz band is a bit more congested than the 5.8GHz band, but both have co-users that you must consider (see Table A-1).

Table A-1. Spectrum allocations for 802.11b and co-users

Part / Use	Start GHz	End GHz
Part 87	0.4700	10.5000
Part 97	2.3900	2.4500
Part 15	2.4000	2.4830
RF lighting	2.4000	2.4835
Part 18	2.4000	2.5000
Part 80	2.4000	9.6000
ISM - 802.11b	2.4010	2.4730
Part 74	2.4500	2.4835
Part 101	2.4500	2.5000
Part 90	2.4500	2.8350
Part 25	5.0910	5.2500
U-NII Low	5.1500	5.2500
U-NII Middle	5.2500	5.3500
Part 97	5.6500	5.9250
U-NII High	5.7250	5.8250
ISM	5.7250	5.8500
Part 18	5.7250	5.8750

The following subsections describe users that you may encounter while deploying 802.11 devices and detail what interference mitigation may be possible for each.

5.2 Devices that Fall into Part 15 of the ISM Band (2400 to 2483 MHz)

This includes unlicensed telecommunications devices such as cordless phones, home spy cameras, and Frequency Hopping (FHSS) or Direct Sequence (DSSS) Spread Spectrum LAN transceivers.

You have neither priority over nor parity with any of these users. Any device that falls into Part 15 must not *cause* harmful interference to all other licensed and legally operating Part 15 users, but it must *accept* interference from all licensed and legally operating Part 15 users. A friend of mine who used to work in the enforcement division of the FCC said, "You have as much right to the band as a garage door opener does."

This is explicitly defined in 15.5:

> 15.5(b) Operation of an intentional, unintentional, or incidental radiator is subject to the conditions that no harmful interference is caused and that interference must be accepted that may be caused by the operation of an authorized radio station, by another intentional or unintentional radiator, by industrial, scientific and medical (ISM) equipment, or by an incidental radiator.

Or basically, everything.

> 15.5(c) The operator of a radio frequency device shall be required to cease operating the device upon notification by a Commission representative that the device is causing harmful interference. Operation shall not resume until the condition causing the harmful interference has been corrected.

Interference objections don't necessarily have to come from a "Commission representative." Operators of other licensed and non-licensed devices can inform you of interference and require that you terminate operation.

Users of 802.11b can interfere with each other even if they are on different channels, as the channels are 22MHz wide and spaced only 5MHz apart. Channels 1, 6, and 11 are the only channels that don't interfere with each other (see Table A-2).

Table A-2. United States 802.11b channel allocations

Channel	Bottom (GHz)	Center (GHz)	Top (GHz)
1	2.401	2.412	2.423
2	2.406	2.417	2.428
3	2.411	2.422	2.433
4	2.416	2.427	2.438
5	2.421	2.432	2.443
6	2.426	2.437	2.448
7	2.431	2.442	2.453
8	2.436	2.447	2.458
9	2.441	2.452	2.463
10	2.446	2.457	2.468
11	2.451	2.462	2.473

5.3   Devices That Fall into the U-NII Band

Unlike the 2.4GHz band, this band does not have overlapping channels. In the lower 200MHz of the U-NII band, there are eight 20MHz-wide channels. You can use any of the channels without interfering with other radios on other channels that are within earshot. Ideally, it's good to know what other Part 15 users are out there. Looking into groups under the banner of "FreeNetworks" is a good place to start.

5.4 Industrial, Scientific, and Medical (ISM) Devices: Part 18

This is also an unlicensed service. Typical ISM applications include the production of physical, biological, or chemical effects such as heating, ionization of gases, mechanical vibrations, hair removal, and the acceleration of charged particles.

Users of this band include ultrasonic devices such as jewelry cleaners, ultrasonic humidifiers, and microwave ovens. Medical devices, such as diathermy equipment and magnetic resonance imaging equipment (MRI) also use ISM, along with some industrial devices such as paint dryers (18.107). RF should be contained within the devices, but other users must accept interference from them.

Part 18 frequencies that could affect 802.11 devices are 2.400 to 2.500GHz and 5.725 to 5.875GHz.

It is difficult to coordinate with the users of Part 18 devices because they are unlicensed and may not realize the impact their equipment has on 802.11 devices.

5.5 Satellite Communications: Part 25

This part of the FCC's rules is applicable to the uplink or downlink of data to and from satellites in Earth orbit. One band that overlaps the U-NII band is reserved for Earth-to-space communications at 5.091 to 5.25GHz. Within this spectrum, 5.091 to 5.150GHz is also allocated to the fixed-satellite service (Earth-to-space), for non-geostationary satellites on a primary basis. The FCC is trying to decommission this band for "feeder" use to satellites. See the "Aviation Services: Part 87" section for details.

Because satellite transmissions involve very narrow aperture antennas pointing into the sky and relatively high power, you are not likely to interfere with them. If you are near one of these installations, there is a very slight chance they could interfere with you.

A note in Part 2.106 [S5.446] allocates 5.150 through 5.216GHz for a similar use: space-to-Earth communications. You have a higher chance of interfering with these installations, because Earth stations deal with very low-level signals from distant satellites.

5.6   Broadcast Auxiliary: Part 74

The traffic on this part of the spectrum normally comes from electronic news gathering (ENG) video links traveling back to studios or television transmitters. Remote news vehicles (such as helicopters and trucks) must be licensed, and only Part 74–eligible entities (usually TV stations) can hold these licenses (74.600).

These transmitters are typically scattered all around an area, as TV remote trucks can go anywhere. Their broadcasts can cause interference to your 802.11 gear, particularly if you're using APs deployed with omni-directional antennas to service an area.

The "receive" points for ENG are often mountain tops and towers. Depending on how 802.11 transmitters are deployed at these same locations, they could cause interference to ENG links. Wireless providers should consider contacting a local frequency coordinator for any Part 74 frequencies that might be affected. The Society of Broadcast Engineers web site (*http://www.sbe.org/*) can provide you with a listing of coordinators for your area.

There have been reports of FHSS devices interfering with these transmissions, because the dwell time for this FHSS tends to punch holes in video links. DSSS is less likely to cause interference to ENG users, but their links can cause problems for your 802.11 deployment.

ENG frequencies that overlap 802.11 devices are 2.450 to 2.467GHz (channel A08) and 2.467 to 2.4835GHz (channel A09) (Part 74.602).

5.7   Stations in the Maritime Services: Part 80

2.4 to 9.6GHz is used for "Radiodetermination," such as RADAR. As with other RADAR users, it is unlikely you will interfere with them. They can interfere with you.

5.8   Aviation Services: Part 87

The frequencies used by this part are for "radio navigation stations" or RADAR. They span the frequencies from 470MHz to 2.450GHz, which overlaps the channels used by 802.11b. They also span 2.450 to 10.500GHz, which overlaps the channels used by 802.11a. It's unlikely that you will ever cause any problems for them. It is far more likely that they will be a nuisance to you.

5.9   Land Mobile Radio Services: Part 90

Users on subpart C of this part can be anyone engaged in a commercial activity. They can use from 2.450 to 2.835GHz, but can license only from 2.450 to 2.483GHz (90.35(a)(3)).

Local government uses subpart B. This includes organizations such as law enforcement, fire departments, etc. Some other uses may include video downlinks for flying platforms such as helicopters, also known as terrestrial surveillance.

> "Even if you are in the right, never argue with someone with a badge and a gun." —Bill Ruck

Even if they are not licensed, official users of this band can put you in jail for interfering with a peace officer in the performance of his duties.

Depending on the commercial or government agency, coordination of this band is performed by different groups, such as the Association of Public Safety Communications Officials (APCO). Consider going to their conferences. You can also try to network with engineering companies that the government uses to outsource frequency coordination.

5.10   Amateur Radio: Part 97

Amateur radio frequencies that overlap 802.11b are found from 2.390 to 2.450GHz. 802.11a is overlapped at 5.650 to 5.925GHz. Amateur users are primary from 2.402 to 2.417GHz and secondary at 2.400 to 2.402GHz.

Amateurs are very protective of their spectrum. The American Radio Relay League (ARRL) is a powerful lobbying force in Washington. They are concerned about all unlicensed devices, and they believe that the FCC doesn't have the right to hand out any part of the spectrum to users of 802.11 devices. You may find that the local groups of amateurs agree and are active with the ARRL's efforts. Getting involved with these local groups and establishing a dialog with them can help minimize interference and avoid conflicts.

5.11   Fixed Microwave Services: Part 101

Users of this band are Local Television Transmission Service (LTTS) and Private Operational Fixed Point-to-Point Microwave Service (POFS). This band is used to transport video. The allocation is from 2.450 to 2.500GHz.

Engineering companies (like CSI Telecommunications) use frequency search companies such as ComSearch to coordinate this part of the spectrum.

5.12   Federal Usage: NTIA/IRAC

The Federal government uses this band for "radiolocation" or "radionavigation." Several warnings in the FCC's Rules and Regulations disclose this fact.

In the case of 802.11b, a note in the Rules warns:

> 15.247(h) Spread spectrum systems are sharing these bands on a noninterference basis with systems supporting critical Government requirements that have been allocated the usage of these bands, secondary only to ISM equipment operated under the provisions of Part 18 of this chapter. Many of these Government systems are airborne radiolocation systems that emit a high EIRP which can cause interference to other users.

The FCC addresses 802.11 with a note in Part 15.407:

> Commission strongly recommends that parties employing U-NII devices to provide critical communications services should determine if there are any nearby Government radar systems that could affect their operation.

Of course, they may not even tell you where such systems are! Coordination is not available, as this band is managed by the NTIA/IRAC. You will need to sniff around using non-802.11 equipment (such a spectrum analyzer) to see what the conditions are.

6   Broadband AUPs

If you depend on cheap broadband connections, you must consider the appropriate use policies (AUPs) of your broadband providers.

6.1   Cable

There are already laws on the books that restrict the sharing of cable bandwidth—cable companies have been dealing with the issue since the birth of their industry in the 1960s. AUPs may not need to spell out restrictions explicitly covering the sharing of Internet access with neighbors. Also, the cable industry specifically has 802.11 on their radar; see *http://www.spectrum.ieee.org/WEBONLY/resource/apr02/webs.html* for details.

Cable providers are scared of NAT, which gives ISP customers the ability to add additional computers to an internal network without applying for additional IP addresses. Cable providers are proposing an alternative to NAT that would allow them to see the actual number of users behind a NAT box and account for a customer's usage of their network.

6.2   Digital Subscriber Line (DSL)

DSL providers are also concerned about oversubscription to their low-cost services. Bandwidth is expensive, and a $50 monthly fee will not cover the cost of a 1.5Mbps DSL going flat-out, 24 hours a day. There is a very good chance that broadband providers will start to charge for extra bandwidth, cap the bandwidth, or be time-sensitive in the usage.

Some Internet providers make no limitations and actually encourage "reselling" of the connection. Normally you will have to pay a premium for this service. Check with the provider for restrictions.

Here's a sample of an AUP with no restrictions:

> TLGNet's TERMS AND CONDITIONS
>
> TLGnet exercises no control whatsoever over the content of the information passing through TLGnet. You are free to communicate commercial, non-commercial, personal, questionable, obnoxious, annoying, or any other kind of information, misinformation, or disinformation through our service. You are fully responsible for the privacy of, content of, and liability for your own communications.
>
> TLGnet exercises no control whatsoever over the content of the information passing through TLGnet. TLGnet makes no warranties of any kind, whether expressed or implied, for the service it is providing. TLGnet also disclaims any warranty of merchantability or fitness for any particular purpose. TLGnet will not be responsible for any damages you suffer or inflict on others. This includes loss resulting from delays, non-deliveries, misdeliveries, or service interruptions caused by its own negligence or your errors or omissions. Use of any information obtained via TLGnet is at your own risk. You are responsible for determining whether or not the traffic you originate will end up being carried on another network, and for following the rules of any such networks. TLGnet specifically denies any responsibility for the accuracy or quality of information obtained through its services.
>
> Any access to other networks connected to TLGnet must comply with the rules appropriate with the other network. Use of TLGnet itself may be for any purpose. Use of TLGnet for commercial purposes is both permitted and encouraged.

7   Human Exposure to Radio Frequency Radiation

I am not going to cover the pseudoscientific arguments of human exposure to radio frequency radiation; I address only the current ANSI limits as related to human exposure to radio frequency fields. However, keep in mind that cellular telephone companies have run into groups that are using this pseudoscience to delay or stop deployment of cell phone installations via city and county governments.

Once 802.11 deployment gets more popular, these groups may have an impact on your deployment. After all, they know what "microwave ovens can do" and 802.11b runs at the same frequency.

The FCC's concern is:

> At the present time there is no federally-mandated radio frequency (RF) exposure standard. However, several non-government organizations, such as the American National Standards Institute (ANSI), the Institute of Electrical and Electronics Engineers Inc. (IEEE), and the National Council on Radiation Protection and Measurements (NCRP) have issued recommendations for human exposure to RF electromagnetic fields.
>
> [...]
>
> On August 1, 1996, the Commission adopted the NCRP's recommended Maximum Permissible Exposure limits for field strength and power density for the transmitters operating at frequencies of 300 KHz to 100 GHz. In addition, the Commission adopted the specific absorption rate (SAR) limits for devices operating within close proximity to the body as specified within the ANSI/IEEE C95.1-1992 guidelines.(See Report and Order, FCC 96-326.) The Commission's requirements are detailed in Parts 1 and 2 of the FCC's Rules and Regulations [47 C.F.R. 1.1307(b), 1.1310, 2.1091, 2.1093].
>
> —From *http://www.fcc.gov/oet/rfsafety*

This breaks down to exposure limits for workers exposed around the equipment and for the general public. At 2.45GHz, it is 4.08mW/cm^2 for unlimited time exposures for workers and 1.63mW/cm^2 for 30 minutes for the general public. As this energy is absorbed over time, you can raise or lower the mW/cm^2 for a controlled situation by decreasing or increasing the time exposed. It would be hard to regulate this in a wireless setup, so you shouldn't apply any "time versus exposure" calculation for the public.

The Office of Engineering and Technology's (OET) Bulletin 65 (August 1997), "Evaluating Compliance With FCC Guidelines for Human Exposure to Radiofrequency Electromagnetic Fields," (*http://www.fcc.gov/oet/info/ documents/bulletins/#65*) shows how to calculate these fields.

For example, a near-field calculation of a two-foot aperture dish (24dBi) with 1/4 watt of power applied (maximum EIRP for point-to-point) results in a one-foot area in front of the dish that is considered "controlled," and a two-foot area (also in front of the dish) where exposure to the general public should be limited. You can comply with these regulations by placing your dishes out of the way; say, above "head height."

The FCC has a page that covers many of these issues at *http://www.fcc.gov/oet/rfsafety/*.

The FCC also has a page on "Cell Phone Facts." This page is designed for end users of RF-emitting equipment and it tries to demystify some of the concerns about RF exposure. You can find the site at *http://www.fda.gov/cellphones/*.

8 Laws Concerning Antennas and Towers

8.1 FCC Preemption of Local Law

When putting up antennas and other gear, you may run into local ordinances and homeowner agreements that are designed to prevent such installations. But, thanks to kind lobbyists like those at the Satellite Broadcasting and Communications Association (SBCA), the FCC has stepped in and overruled most of these local ordinances and agreements.

For a good introduction to this topic, read Roy Trumbell's paper at *http://www.lns.com/sbe/antenna_mounts.html*.

This rule should apply only to broadcast signals such as TV, DBS, or MMDS. However, it might be argued that the provision for MMDS could also cover wireless data deployment, because:

> 1.4000 Restrictions impairing reception of television broadcast signals, direct broadcast satellite services, or multichannel multipoint distribution services:
>
> 1.4000(a)(1)(i) An antenna that is:
>
> (A) Used to receive direct broadcast satellite service, including direct-to-home satellite service, or to receive or transmit fixed wireless signals via satellite, and
>
> (B) One meter or less in diameter or is located in Alaska;
>
> [...]
>
> 1.4000(a)(2) For purposes of this section, "fixed wireless signals" means any commercial non-broadcast communications signals transmitted via wireless technology to and/or from a fixed customer location. Fixed wireless signals do not include, among other things, AM radio, FM radio, amateur (HAM) radio, Citizen's Band (CB) radio, and Digital Audio Radio Service (DARS) signals.

There are conditions:

> 1.400(c) In the case of an antenna that is used to transmit fixed wireless signals, the provisions of this section shall apply only if a label is affixed to the antenna that:
>
> (1) Provides adequate notice regarding potential radiofrequency safety hazards, e.g., information regarding the safe minimum separation distance required between users and transceiver antennas; and
>
> (2) References the applicable FCC-adopted limits for radiofrequency exposure specified in 1.1310 of this chapter.

Issues such as "can traffic such as Multicast IP fall under these rules?" and "what percentage of traffic must be broadcast?" need to be resolved before this section of the FCC rules can be fully interpreted.

8.2   Height Limitations

8.2.1   Local ordinances

Most cities regulate the construction of towers. These regulations are all different, but maximum height limits are usually given (e.g., 300 feet for a tower in Oakland, or 10 feet for a mast on a residence in Fremont), zoning considerations (residential or commercial) apply, construction specifications (no antennas 15 feet above a tower in Oakland, or a 300-foot setback in Fremont) must be followed, and aesthetic limitations (e.g., what color, how hidden) are always a factor. You will have to jump over various hurdles with each city and installation.

8.2.2   FAA and FCC tower registration

The FAA is very concerned about tall structures that airplanes could bump into. Part 17.7(a) of the FCC R&R defines these structures as:

> Any construction or alteration of more than 60.96 meters (200 feet) in height above ground level at its site.

The next section details which towers must be marked, and gives special attention to structures that may be in the glide slope of a runway or pose "extraordinary hazard potentials."

Details can also be found in the U.S. Department of Transportation Advisory Circular AC70/7460-1K.

If your tower falls into this category, you must register it with the FCC, per Part 17.4.

9   The Future: Good News and Bad News

What innovations can we look forward to, and what problems might we face?

9.1   Good News: New Standards to Help

Standards that allow coexistence between current and upcoming protocols are in development.

9.1.1   802.11h

This IEEE group (802.11h) is developing transmission power control (TPC) and dynamic frequency selection (DFS) protocols. These protocols will use the band more efficiently and be required for European deployment.

The standard is expected to be available soon. Atheros Communications, Inc. is already starting to ship 802.11a chipsets with these features.

9.1.2   802.15: WPAN (Bluetooth)

The 802.15 IEEE task group is developing a set of "Coexistence Mechanisms" that will facilitate the coexistence of WLAN and WPAN devices with methods such as "Data Rate Scaling."

9.1.3   802.16.2

The subgroup of "Working Group on Broadband Wireless Access Standards" for Metropolitan Area Networks (MANs) is called "Coexistence of Fixed Broadband Wireless Access Systems." This group is researching what it takes to deploy a MAN and to solve interference issues.

9.2   The Bad News

New sources of interference and organized opposition to wireless community networks may make deployment more difficult.

9.2.1   Radio frequency (RF) lighting

Some companies have experimented with excited sodium lamps that use RF energy from 2.4 to 2.4835GHz. Such lamps have a broader and more contiguous spectrum than mercury vapor. They are also four times more efficient.

ISM band users are concerned that this type of lamp could add considerable noise to the 2.4GHz band. Short- and long-range 802.11b could be crippled.

9.2.2 Will other folks try to shut down 802.11, or will they accept it?

The ARRL is very active in commenting on proposed rules that would give more spectrum to unlicensed users. They are particularly concerned about spectrum that is currently used by amateurs. Some insight can be gained at the ARRL's page on Part 15 devices at *http://www.arrl.org/tis/info/part15.html*.

The NTIA/IRAC is concerned about this spectrum, because they also use it. However, the exact use may be secret; it isn't really defined anymore than "radionavigation" (read: RADAR). They are also very concerned about future Ultra Wide Band developments and have sent out a number of "hand slaps" to the FCC for their recent rulemaking on UWB. It is likely that they see the ISM and U-NII bands for what they are and have given up on it and moved any low EIRP communications from it.

Some people are also concerned that 3G license holders may be actively working against 802.11 use, which can be seen as very cheap competition to the very expensive 3G spectrum development and deployment. We haven't seen anything definitive, but keep an eye on this possible conflict.

10   What Can You Do?

If any group or individual wanted to shut down long-distance 802.11 use, they could do it via the FCC's Rules and Regulations, or by creating new rules that encourage FCC enforcement of the current rules on owner restrictions and equipment certification. If you are concerned about this lobbying, subscribe to the emailed daily reports from the FCC at *http://www.fcc.gov/Daily_Releases/Daily_Digest/*.

It's also helpful to know how to comment on Notices of Inquiry (NOI) or Notices of Proposed Rulemaking (NPRM). The FCC has public comment periods for both items, but it is up to you to find out about changes that might affect you. Once you've researched the issue, submit a good argument that describes why you do or don't want a particular NPRM to become a new rule. A good page covering NOIs, NPRMs, and the process of commenting to the FCC can be found in the "How Do I..." section of the FCC's web site (*http://wireless.fcc.gov/csinfo/*).

11   Conclusions

- Building a business on Part 15 spectrum has risks; you have no priority over anyone else.

- Coordination with other users (i.e., Parts 15, 74, 90, and 101) can extend the life of a network.

- A properly engineered and designed network will live longer than one that isn't properly designed. However, a well-built network may still have a limited lifetime if there is an increase in noise or interference from other users.

- Other users may try to stifle 802.11 communication by suggesting changes to the FCC Rules and Regulations. A well-coordinated effort that tracks and responds to proposed rules detrimental to Part 15 users is needed. WISP organizations or the loosely coordinated networks of FreeNetworks.org might be able to provide some assistance in this area.

Path Loss Calculations

Here is a simple table of path loss calculations in free space for channel 1 with clear line of sight (the difference in path loss from channel 1 to channel 11 is negligible). See Chapter 6 shows how to use these numbers to figure out how far your network can reach. Distances are in miles; losses are in dB.

Distance (in miles)	Losses on channel 1 (in dB)
0.5	98
1	104
2	110
3	114
4	116
5	118
7	121
10	124
15	128
20	130
25	132
30	134

The path loss table above was calculated with the following formula, rounded up to the nearest whole number:

$$L = 20 \log(d) + 20 \log(f) + 36.6$$

Check out ARRL online (*http://www.arrl.org*) for what might be the most authoritative source of radio information on the planet. Their excellent books (in particular, *UHF/Microwave Experimenter's Manual* and *The ARRL Antenna Book*) are the definitive sources for learning about microwave communications.

Simple Scheme Management

This is a simple method for managing your network schemes on Linux. You will need *sudo* installed. Use sudo privileges to run */sbin/cardctl*, then create the following shell script called *scheme*:

```
#!/bin/sh

SCHEME=`/usr/bin/basename $0`

if [ "$SCHEME" == "scheme" ]; then
  unset SCHEME
fi

/usr/bin/sudo /sbin/cardctl scheme $SCHEME
```

Install the script somewhere in your PATH (I put mine in *~/bin*). Then make symlinks to the script with the names of schemes you want to access quickly, in the same directory:

```
rob@entropy:~/bin$ ln -s scheme home
rob@entropy:~/bin$ ln -s scheme oreilly
rob@entropy:~/bin$ ln -s scheme nocat
rob@entropy:~/bin$ ln -s scheme any
```

Now make matching entries in your */etc/pcmcia/wireless.opts*:

```
home,*,*,*)
    INFO="IBSS net at Home"
    ESSID="HomeNet"
    MODE="Ad-Hoc"
    KEY="1234-5678-90"
    RATE="11M"
    ;;

oreilly,*,*,*)
    INFO="Work"
    ESSID="OReillyNet"
    MODE="Managed"
```

```
        KEY="s:sHHHH"
        IWCONFIG="power unicast"
        ;;

nocat,*,*,*)
        INFO="NoCat Community net"
        ESSID="NoCat"
        MODE="Managed"
        ;;

any,*,*,*)
        INFO="Default configuration"
        ESSID="ANY"
        MODE="Managed"
        ;;
```

When you want to change schemes quickly, just type *home* or *any* to instantly change all of your wireless and network settings. As an added bonus, typing *scheme* shows the current scheme. Keep in mind that *sudo* will prompt you for your password—you need to be root to change the scheme.

Index

We'd like to hear your suggestions for improving our indexes. Send email to *index@oreilly.com*.

Wi-Fi, 20
wired equivalent privacy (see WEP)
wireless
    cost, 9, 13
    hardware requirements, 13
    range, 9
wireless client bridge, 24
wireless communities list
    Bay Area Wireless Users Group
       (BAWUG), 122
    BC Wireless, 125
    communities web site, 121
    Consume, 126
    Houston Wireless, 125
    Melbourne Wireless, 126
    NYCwireless, 124
    PersonalTelco, 123
    RedLibre, 127
    Seattle Wireless, 122
    Wireless Leiden, 127
wireless cooperatives, 6
wireless discovery tool, 94
Wireless Distribution System
    (WDS), 110

Wireless DSL, 5
wireless gateway, 52
Wireless HOWTO web site, 53
wireless in Sebastopol, 129–136
Wireless Internet Service Provider (see
    WISP)
Wireless Leiden, 127
wireless networking standard, de
    facto, 10
wireless networks around the
    globe, 121–128
wireless router-on-a-floppy (WRP), 134
Wireless Tools package web site, 62
wireless utopia, 8
WISP, 4–6
WLAN Service Area ID, 23
wound helical antenna, 106
    web site, 106
WPAN, 154

Y

yagi antennas, 79, 98

About the Author

Rob Flickenger is a writer and editor for O'Reilly by day and an all-around hack almost all of the time. He enjoys fiddling around with puzzles and creating machines that make electrons dance. Entertained by the usual complement of obscure British sci-fi and humor, he has endless fun trying to comprehend the Nature of Human Existence and his Place in the Universe, all while living with multiple cats and battling a fierce addiction to the coffee drinks of Northern California. He truly believes that "infinite free bandwidth everywhere" is a design goal, not a fantasy.

Colophon

Our look is the result of reader comments, our own experimentation, and feedback from distribution channels. Distinctive covers complement our distinctive approach to technical topics, breathing personality and life into potentially dry subjects.

The animal on the cover of *Building Wireless Community Networks*, Second Edition is a Carolina parakeet, *Conuropsis carolinensis*, the only parrot native to the United States. These foot-long, multicolored birds, with their green bodies and yellow and orange heads and necks, were voracious eaters of fruit and grain seeds. This behavior led to their wholesale destruction as agricultural pests. Although they were once found all over the southeastern United States, the last known Carolina parakeet died in the Cincinnati Zoo on February 21, 1918.

Philip Dangler was the production editor and copyeditor for *Building Wireless Community Networks*, Second Edition. Genevieve d'Entremont was the proofreader. Emily Quill and Darren Kelly provided quality control. Reg Aubry wrote the index. Jamie Peppard provided production assistance.

Ellie Volckhausen designed the cover of this book, based on a series design by Edie Freedman. The cover image is a 19th-century engraving from the Dover Pictorial Archive. Emma Colby produced the cover layout with QuarkXPress 4.1 using Adobe's ITC Garamond font.

David Futato designed the interior layout. Joe Wizda converted the files from Microsoft Word to FrameMaker 5.5.6 using tools created by Mike Sierra. The text font is Linotype Birka; the heading font is Adobe Myriad Condensed; and the code font is LucasFont's TheSans Mono Condensed. The illustrations that appear in the book were produced by Robert Romano and Jessamyn Read using Macromedia FreeHand 9 and Adobe Photoshop 6. The tip and warning icons were drawn by Christopher Bing. This colophon was written by Leanne Soylemez.

ther Titles Available from O'Reilly

ork Administration

DNS and BIND, 4th Edition

By Paul Albitz & Cricket Liu
4th Edition April 2001
622 pages, ISBN 0-596-00158-4

DNS and BIND, 4th Edition, covers BIND 9, which implements many new and important features, as well as BIND 8, on mercial products are based. extensive coverage of NOTIFY, and reverse mapping, transaction signew DNS Security Extensions; accommodating Windows 2000 and Domain Controllers.

DNS & BIND Cookbook

By Cricket Liu
1st Edition October 2002
240 pages, ISBN 0-596-00410-9

The *DNS & BIND Cookbook* presents solutions to the many problems faced by network administrators responsible for a s title is an indispensable compan-*IND*, 4th Edition, the definitive al task of name server adminis-ookbook contains dozens of code solutions to everyday problems, mple questions, like, "How do I get advanced topics like providing IPv6 addresses.

Network Troubleshooting Tools

By Joseph D. Sloan
1st Edition August 2001
364 pages, ISBN 0-596-00186-X

Network Troubleshooting Tools helps you sort through the thousands of tools that have been developed for debugging TCP/IP hoose the ones that are best for so shows you how to approach shooting using these tools, how to network so you know how it rmal conditions, and how to oblems when they arise so you can effectively.

TCP/IP Network Administration, 3rd Edition

By Craig Hunt
3rd Edition April 2002
746 pages, ISBN 0-596-00297-1

This complete hands-on guide to setting up and running a TCP/IP network starts with the fundamentals: what protocols do and how they work, how addresses and routing are used, and how to set up your network connection. The book also covers advanced routing protocols and provides tutorials on configuring important network services. The expanded third edition includes sections on Samba, Apache web server, network security, and much more.

Managing NFS and NIS, 2nd Edition

By Hal Stern, Mike Eisler & Ricardo Labiaga
2nd Edition July 2001
510 pages, ISBN 1-56592-510-6

This long-awaited new edition of a classic, now updated for NFS Version 3 and based on Solaris 8, shows how to set up and manage a network filesystem installation. *Managing NFS and NIS* is the only practical book devoted entirely to NFS and the distributed database NIS; it's a "must-have" for anyone interested in Unix networking.

sendmail, 3rd Edition

By Bryan Costales with Eric Allman
3rd Edition December 2002
1232 pages, ISBN 1-56592-839-3

Versions 8.10 through 8.12 of the sendmail program differ so significantly from earlier versions that a massive rewrite of our best-selling reference was called for. With so many web sites now seeking to make mail delivery efficient, there's a new chapter on performance tuning, and because sendmail 8.10 and above are now rich in anti-spam features, a chapter on handling spam has been added. Also new to this edition is coverage of other programs supplied with sendmail, such as vacation and makemap. These additional programs are pivotal to sendmail's daily operation. Altogether, versions 8.10 through 8.12 include dozens of new features, options, and macros, and this greatly expanded edition thoroughly addresses each.

ork Administration

802.11 Security

By Bruce Potter & Bob Fleck
1st Edition December 2002
182 pages, ISBN 0-596-00290-4

This book shows how to secure
802.11-based wireless networks
focusing particularly on the
802.11b specification. Includes
of security issues unique to wire-
uch as Wireless Access Points
h stealing, and the problematic
alent Privacy component of 802.11.
w to configure a wireless client
P using either Linux or FreeBSD.
ork access and encrypting client
vered thoroughly.

BGP

By Iljitsch van Beijnum
1st Edition September 2002
288 pages, ISBN 0-596-00254-8

This handy book addresses the
BGP protocol in two practical
ways. First, it provides information
that will allow managers and
ators to assess whether having
ions to the Internet and using BGP
ion for their organization. The
he pros and cons of BGP, along
es of routing packets all over the
BGP handles that complexity.

Practical VoIP Using Vocal

By David G. Kelly, Cullen Jennings
& Luan Dang
1st Edition July 2002
528 pages, ISBN 0-596-00078-2

While many books describe the
theory behind Voice over IP, only
this one describes how such a
as actually built, and how you too
source code, install it onto a sys-
hones, and make calls. Because
source, you can look "under the
how the system works, and how
oblems are being worked out in the
ronment.

802.11 Wireless Networks: The Definitive Guide

By Matthew Gast
1st Edition April 2002
464 pages, 0-596-00183-5

As a network administrator,
architect, or security professional, you need to understand the
capabilities, limitations, and risks associated with
integrating wireless LAN technology into your
current infrastructure. This practical guide provides all the information necessary to analyze and
deploy wireless networks with confidence. It's the
only source that offers a full spectrum view of
802.11, from the minute details of the specification,
to deployment, monitoring, and troubleshooting.

RADIUS

By Jonathan Hassell
1st Edition September 2002
206 pages, ISBN 0-596-00322-6

This new book provides a complete, detailed guide into the
underpinnings of the RADIUS
protocol, with particular empha-
sis on the utility of user accounting. Author
Jonathan Hassell also provides practical suggestions for using an open-source variation called
FreeRADIUS, giving the reader background in
both RADIUS theory and practice.

O'REILLY NETWORK

Safari® Bookshelf™

Search Over 1,000 Books and
Find Answers Fast

The Safari Bookshelf is a powerful online reference tool, a must when you need to pinpoint exact answers in an instant. With access to over 1000 of the top technical reference books leading publishers including O'Reilly, Addison-Wesley, and the Microsoft Press, Safari Bookshelf provides developers with the technical reference and code samples needed to develop timely code.

How to stay in touch with O'Reilly

ard-winning web site

http://www.oreilly.com/

ites on the Web"—PC Magazine
gazine's Web Business 50 Awards

contains a library of comprehen-
nformation (including book
tables of contents), downloadable
kground articles, interviews with
aders, links to relevant sites, book
and more. File us in your bookmarks

Join our email mailing lists

t email announcements of new
nferences, special offers, and
work technology newsletters at:

eilly.com

ustomize your free elists subscription
xactly the O'Reilly news you want.

xamples from our books

ample files for a book, go to:

eilly.com/catalog

book, and follow the "Examples" link.

ork with us

r web site for current
opportunites:

eilly.com/

our book

book at:
.oreilly.com

6. Contact us

O'Reilly & Associates, Inc.
1005 Gravenstein Hwy North
Sebastopol, CA 95472 USA
TEL: 707-827-7000 or 800-998-9938
        (6am to 5pm PST)
FAX: 707-829-0104

order@oreilly.com
For answers to problems regarding your order
or our products. To place a book order online
visit:

http://www.oreilly.com/order_new/

catalog@oreilly.com
To request a copy of our latest catalog.

booktech@oreilly.com
For book content technical questions or
corrections.

corporate@oreilly.com
For educational, library, government, and
corporate sales.

proposals@oreilly.com
To submit new book proposals to our editors
and product managers.

international@oreilly.com
For information about our international distributors or translation queries. For a list of
our distributors outside of North America
check out:

http://international.oreilly.com/distributors.html

adoption@oreilly.com
For information about academic use of
O'Reilly books, visit:

http://academic.oreilly.com